AII
TAIL (

590 colour illustrations to aid in the quick recognition of airlines

B I HENGI

Midland Publishing

Entry explanation:

[1] **ACES COLUMBIA**
[2] AES : Aces [3]
[4] HK : CLM [5]
[6] AT4 : DHT : 72M : 72S

[1] Airline name

[2] Three-letter code
– used by airline for
flight numbers etc.

[3] Radio call sign prefix.

[4] International aircraft
registration prefix.

[5] ITU Country code
(see pages 153-155).

[6] Aircraft types used –
IATA codes
(see pages 3-5).

Airline Tail Colours second edition
© 2000 Midland Publishing and NARA-Verlag

ISBN 1 85780 104 0

This English language edition published 2000 by
Midland Publishing,
24 The Hollow, Earl Shilton,
Leicester, LE9 7NA, England.
Telephone: 01455 847 815 Fax: 01455 841 805
E-mail: midlandbooks@compuserve.com

Midland Publishing is an imprint of
Ian Allan Publishing Ltd

Also published in 2000 in German by
NARA-Verlag, Postfach 1241,
D-85388 Allershausen, Germany,
as 'Airline-Kennung'

Worldwide distribution (except North America):
Midland Counties Publications
Unit 3 Maizefield, Hinckley Fields,
Hinckley, Leics., LE10 1YF, England.
Telephone: 01455 233 747 Fax: 01455 233 737
E-mail: midlandbooks@compuserve.com

North American trade distribution:
Specialty Press Publishers and Wholesalers
11605 Kost Dam Road, North Branch, MN 55056, USA
Telephone: 651 583 3239 Fax: 651 583 2023
Toll free telephone: 800 895 4585

Design concept and layout
© 2000 Midland Publishing and NARA-Verlag

Printed in Hong Kong

Aircraft Type Abbreviations (IATA-codings)

ABF	Airbus Industrie A300-600C Freighter	**CWC**	Curtiss C-46 Commando
AB2	Airbus Industrie A300-B2	**DC3**	Douglas DC-3
AB3	Airbus Industrie A300	**DC4**	Douglas DC-4
AB6	Airbus Industrie A300-600B	**DC6**	Douglas DC-6
A6F	Airbus Industrie A300-600ST 'Beluga'	**DC8**	Douglas DC-8
		DC9	Douglas DC-9
ACD	Rockwell Commander	**DHO**	de Havilland DHC-3 Otter
AN4	Antonov An-24	**DHP**	de Havilland DHC-2 Beaver
AN6	Antonov An-26/32	**DHT**	de Havilland DHC-6 Twin Otter
AN7	Antonov An-70/72	**DH4**	de Havilland DHC-4 Caribou
ANF	Antonov An-12	**DH7**	de Havilland DHC-7
ARJ	Avro Intl. Aerospace Avroliner (All series)	**DH8**	de Havilland DHC-8 Dash 8 (All series)
ATP	British Aerospace ATP	**D1C**	McDonnell Douglas DC-10
AT2	Aérospatiale/Alenia ATR-42-200/300	**D1F**	McDonnell Douglas DC-10 Freighter
AT4	Aérospatiale/Alenia ATR-42-500	**D1M**	McDonnell Douglas DC-10 Combi
AT7	Aérospatiale/Alenia ATR-72	**D10**	McDonnell Douglas DC-10 (All series)
ATR	Aérospatiale/Alenia ATR (All series)		
A4F	Antonov An-124 Ruslan Freighter	**D28**	Fairchild/Dornier 228
BE1	Beechcraft 1900 (All series)	**D38**	Fairchild/Dornier 328
BNI	Britten Norman Islander	**D3F**	Douglas DC-3/C-47 Freighter
BNT	Britten Norman Trislander	**D6F**	Douglas DC-6 Freighter
B11	British Aerospace (BAC) 1-11 (All series)	**D8F**	McDonnell DC-8 Freighter
B15	British Aerospace (BAC) 1-11-500 (All series)	**D8M**	McDonnell Douglas DC-8 Combi
		D8S	McDonnell Douglas DC-8 (Series 60 and 70)
CD2	GAF N22/N24 Nomad	**D9F**	McDonnell Douglas DC-9 Freighter
CL4	Canadair CL-44		
CNA	Cessna (All series, Prop/Turboprop)	**D9S**	McDonnell Douglas DC-9 (Series 30, 40, 50 and 80)
CRJ	Canadair Regional Jet	**EMB**	Embraer EMB 110 Bandeirante
CRV	Aérospatiale Caravelle (All series)	**EM2**	Embraer EMB 120 Brasilia
		EM3	Embraer EMB 135
CS2	CASA/Nusantara 212 Aviocar	**EM4**	Embraer EMB 145
CS5	CASA/Nusantara 235	**FK7**	Fairchild FH-227
CVF	Convair 440/580/600/640 Freighter	**F27**	Fokker F.27 Friendship
		F28	Fokker F.28 Fellowship (All series)
CVR	Convair (All passenger series)	**F50**	Fokker 50

F70	Fokker 70	SWM	Fairchild-Swearingen
GRG	Grumman Goose		Metro/Merlin
GRJ	Gulfstream 11/111/1V	S20	Saab 2000
GRM	Grumman Mallard	TU3	Tupolev Tu-134
GRS	Gulfstream 1/1-C	TU5	Tupolev Tu-154
HPH	Handley Page Dart Herald	T20	Tupolev Tu-204
HS7	British Aerospace HS.748	VCV	Vickers Viscount
ILW	Ilyushin IL-86	YK2	Yakolev Yak- 42
IL4	Ilyushin IL-114	YK4	Yakolev Yak-40
IL6	Ilyushin IL-62/62M	YN2	Yunshuji 12
IL7	Ilyushin IL-76	YN5	Yunshuji 5
IL8	Ilyushin IL-18	YN7	Yunshuji 7
IL9	Ilyushin IL-96/IL-96M	YS1	NAMC YS-11
J31	British Aerospace Jetstream 31	100	Fokker 100
J41	British Aerospace Jetstream 41	14F	British Aerospace 146 Freighter
LOE	Lockheed L-188 Electra	146	British Aerospace 146
LOF	Lockheed L-188 Electra Freighter		(All passenger series)
LOH	Lockheed L-100 Hercules	310	Airbus Industrie A 310
	Freighter		(All passenger series)
LOM	Lockheed L-188 Electra Combi	313	Airbus Industrie A 310-300
L1F	Lockheed TriStar Freighter	32S	Airbus Industrie A 320
L10	Lockheed L-1011 TriStar		(All series)
	(All series)	320	Airbus Industrie A 320-200
L15	Lockheed L-1011 TriStar-500	321	Airbus Industrie A 321
L4T	LET-410 Turbolet	319	Airbus Industrie A 319
M1F	McDonnell Douglas MD-11	330	Airbus Industrie A 330
	Freighter	332	Airbus Industrie A 330-200
M1M	McDonnell Douglas MD-11	333	Airbus Industrie A 330-300
	Combi	340	Airbus Industrie A 340
M11	McDonnell Douglas MD-11	342	Airbus Industrie A 340-200
M80	McDonnell Douglas MD-80	343	Airbus Industrie A 340-300
	(All series)	345	Airbus Industrie A 340-500
M82	McDonnell Douglas MD-82	346	Airbus Industrie A 340-600
M83	McDonnell Douglas MD-83	70F	Boeing 707 Freighter
M87	McDonnell Douglas MD-87	707	Boeing 707
M90	McDonnell Douglas MD-90		(All passenger series)
ND2	Aérospatiale N262/Mohawk 298	717	Boeing 717
SF3	Saab SF 340	712	Boeing 717-200
SHB	Shorts SC.5 Belfast	72F	Boeing 727 Freighter
SHS	Shorts Skyvan	72M	Boeing 727 Combi
SH3	Shorts 330	72S	Boeing 727-200 Passenger
SH6	Shorts 360	727	Boeing 727 (All series)
SSC	Aérospatiale-BAC Concorde	73F	Boeing 737-200 Freighter

73G	Boeing 737-700	**743**	Boeing 747-300
73M	Boeing 737-200 Combi	**744**	Boeing 747-400
73S	Boeing 737-200 Passenger	**747**	Boeing 747
733	Boeing 737-300/300/QC		(All passenger series)
734	Boeing 737-400	**75F**	Boeing 757 Freighter
735	Boeing 737-500	**757**	Boeing 757-200
736	Boeing 737-600	**753**	Boeing 757-300
737	Boeing 737	**76F**	Boeing 767 Freighter
	(All passenger series)	**762**	Boeing 767-200
738	Boeing 737-800	**763**	Boeing 767-300/300E
74D	Boeing 747-300 Combi	**764**	Boeing 767-400
74E	Boeing 747-400 Combi	**767**	Boeing 767 (All series)
74F	Boeing 747 Freighter (All series)	**772**	Boeing 777-200
74L	Boeing 747 SP	**773**	Boeing 777-300
74M	Boeing 747-200 Combi	**777**	Boeing 777

Photographic acknowledgements

Special thanks are due to Albert Kuhbandner who has provided a substantial portion of the photos for this new edition. Other shots are from the archives of the author, as well as from Martin Bach, Uwe Gleisberg, Josef Krauthäuser, Patrick Lutz and Dennis Wehrmann.

ABOITIZ AIR
BOI : Abair
RP : PHL
YS1 : LOH

ACES COLOMBIA
AES : Aces
HK : CLM
AT4 : DHT : 32S : 72M : 72S

ADC AIRLINES
ADK : Adco
5N : NIG
70F : 72S

ADRIA AIRWAYS
ADR : Adria
S5 : SVN
32S : CRJ

AEGEAN AIRLINES
AEE : Aegean
SX : GRC
ARJ : 100

AER LINGUS
EIN : Shamrock
EI : IRL
321 : 32S : 333 : 146 : F50 : 734 :
735

AERO CARIBBEAN
CRN : Aerocaribbean
CU : CUB
AN4 : AN6 : AT4 : IL8 : YK4

AEROCALIFORNIA
SER : Aerocalifornia
XA : MEX
DC9

AEROCARIBE
CBE : Aerocaribe
XA : MEX
DC9 : FK7 : J31

AERO CONTINENTE
ACQ : Aero Continente
OB : PRU
F27 : F28 : 737 : 727

**AEROFLOT - RUSSIAN
INTERNATIONAL AIRLINES**
AFL : Aeroflot
RA : RUS
IL6 : IL7 : ILW : TU3 : TU5 : 313 :
D1F : 734 : 767 : 777

AEROGAVIOTA
GTV : Gaviota
CU : CUB
AN4 : AN6 : AT4 : YK4

**AEROLINAS
ARGENTINAS**
ARG : Argentina
LV : ARG
M80 : 73S : 747 : 340

AEROLITORAL
SLI : Costera
XA : MEX
SWM : SF3

AERO LLOYD
AEF : Aerolloyd
D : D
M80 : 32S : 321

AEROLYON
AEY : Aerolyon
F : F
D10

AEROMAR AIRLINES
ROM : Bravo Quebec
HI : DOM
DC6 : 72S

AEROMAR
TAO : Trans-Aeromar
XA : MEX
AT2 : AT4

AEROMEXICO
AMX : Aeromexico
XA : MEX
DC9 : M80 : M87 : 757 : 762 : 763

AEROPOSTAL
LAV : Aeropostal
YV : VEN
DC9 : 32S

AEROREPUBLICA
RPB : Aerorepublica
HK : CLM
DC9 : 727

AEROSUCRE
KRE : Aerosucre
HK : CLM
CRV : 727

AEROSUR
ASU : Aerosur
CP : BOL
72S : YK4

AER TURAS
ATT : Aerturas
EI : IRL
L10 : D8F

13

AFRICAN INTERNATIONAL
AIA : Fly Cargo
3D : SWZ
D8F

AIR 2000
AMM : Jetset
G : GB
32S : 321 : 332 : 757 : 763

AIR AFRIQUE
RKA : Airafric
TU : CTI *
AB4 : AB6 : 313 : D10 : 70F : 73S

AIR ALFA YOLLARI
LFA : Air Alfa
TC : TUR
321

AIR ALGERIE
DAH : Air Algerie
7T : ALG
CNA : 310 : 73S : 72S : 767 :
F27 : LOH

AIR ALM
ALM : Antillean
PJ : ATN
DH8 : M80

AIR ARUBA
ARU : Aruba
P4 : NA
DC9 : M80 : M90

AIR ASIA
AXM : Asian Express
9M : MLA
733

AIR ATLANTA ICELAND
ABD : Atlanta
TF : ISL
747 : L10

AIR ATLANTIQUE
APB : Charente
F : F
AT2

AIR BALTIC
BTI : Airbaltic
YL : LVA
ARJ : F50 : SF3

AIR BELGIUM
ABB : Air Belgium
OO : BEL
734

AIR BERLIN
BER : Air Berlin
D : D
734 : 738

AIR BOTNIA
KFB : Botnia
OH : FIN
F28 : J31 : SF3

AIR BOTSWANA
BOT : Botswana
A2 : BOT
AT4 : 146

AIRBUS TRANSPORT INTERNATIONAL
BGA : Super Transport
F : F
A6F

AIR CAIRO
— : Air Cairo
SU : EGY
T20

AIR CALEDONIE
TPC : Aircal
F : NCL
AT4 : D28

AIR CANADA
ACA : Air Canada
C : CAN
CRJ : DC9 : 319 : 32S : 340 :
767 : 763 747 : 744

AIR CHINA INTERNATIONAL
CCA : Air China
B : CHN
YN2 : YN7 : 146 : 343 : 733 :
738 : 747 : 74L : 744 : 767 : 763 :
772 : LOH

AIR CARIBBEAN
CBB : Ibis
9Y : TRD
YS1 : 73S

AIR CONTRACTORS
ABR : Contract
EI : IRL
72F : AB4

AIR CREEBEC
CRQ : Cree
C : CAN
BE1 : EMB : DH8 : HS7

AIR DOLOMITI
DLA : Dolomiti
I : I
AT2 : AT4 : AT7 : F100

AIR DJIBOUTI
DJU : Air Djib
J2 : DJI
310

AIR EUROPA
AEA : Aireuropa
EC : E
733 : 734 : 757 : 762 : 763

AIR EUROPA EXPRESS
AEA : Aireuropa Express
EC : E
ATP

AIR EUROPE
AEL : Air Europe
I : I
32S : 763 : 772

AIR FRANCE
AFR : Airfrans
F : F
AB3 : 310 : 313 : 319 : 32S : 321 :
340 : 343 : 73S : 733 : 735 : 763 :
74F : 747 : 744 : 74M : 772 : SSC

AIR GABON
AGN : Golf November
TR : GAB
72S : 73S : 747 : F28

AIR GREAT WALL
CGW : Changcheng
B : CHN
73S

AIR GREECE
AGJ : Air Greece
SX : GRC
AT7 : 100

AIR GUADELOUPE
AGU : Air Guadeloupe
F : F-GDL
AT4 : AT7 : DHT : D28 : 73S

AIR HOLLAND
AHR : Orange
PH : HOL
733

AIR HONGKONG
AHK : Air Hongkong
B-H : HKG
74F

AIR INUIT
AIE : Air Inuit
C : CAN
CVF : DHT : DH8 : HS7

AIR JAMAICA
AJM : Juliet Mike
6Y : JMC
313 : 343 : 32S : 321

AIR JAMAICA EXPRESS
JMX : Jamaica Express
6Y : JMC
D28 : SH6

AIR JET
AIJ : Airjet
F : F
146

AIR KAZAKSTAN
KZK : Air Kazakstan
UN : KAZ
AN4 : IL7 : ILW : TU3 : TU5 : 73S

AIR KORYO
KCA : Airkoryo
P : KRE
AN4 : IL6 : IL7 : IL8 : TU3 : TU5

AIR LABRADOR
LAL : Labair
C : CAN
DHO : DHT : DH8 : SH3 : SH6

AIR LIBERTE
LIB : Liberté
F : F
MD8 : D10 : F28 : 100

AIR LITHUANIA
KLA : KLA
LY : LTU
AT4 : TU3 : YK4

AIR LITTORAL
LIT : Air Littoral
F : F
AT4 : BE1 : CRJ : EM2 : F70 : 100

AIR MACAU
AMU : Air Macau
B-M : MAC
32S : 321

AIR MADAGASCAR
MDG : Madair
5R : MDG
73S : 733 : 747 : 763 : DHT : HS7

AIR MALAWI
AML : Malawi
7Q : MWI
AT4 : D28 : 733

AIR MALDIVES
AMI : Air Maldives
8Q : MLD
DH8 : D28 : 310

AIR MALTA
AMC : Air Malta
9H : MLT
32S : 73S : 733 : 734

AIR MANDALAY
— : Air Mandalay
XY : BRM
AT7

AIR MARSHALL ISLANDS
MRS : Marshallislands
V7 : MRL
D28 : HS7 : S20

AIR MAURITANIE
MRT : Air Mauretania
5T : MTN
F28

AIR MAURITIUS
MAU : Airmauritius
3B : MAU
AT4 : 343 : 767

AIR MEDITERRANEE
BIE : Mediterranée
F : F
73S

AIR MOLDOVA
MLD : Air Moldova
ER : MDA
A24 : A26 : TU3

**AIR MOLDOVA
INTERNATIONAL**
MLV : Moldovainternational
ER : MDA
A24 : Y40 : Y42

AIR NAMIBIA
NMB : Namibair
V5 : NMB
BE1 : 73S : 74E

AIR NAURU
RON : Air Nauru
C2 : NRU
734

AIR NEW ZEALAND
ANZ : New Zealand
ZK : NZL
73S : 733 : 747 : 744 : 762 : 763

AIR NIPPON
ANK : Ankair
JA : J
32S : 73S : 735 : DHT : YS1

AIR NIUGINI
ANG : Niugini
P2 : PNG
DH8 : F28 : 146

AIR NORTH
ANT : Airnorth
C - CF : CAN
BE9 : DC3 : HS7

AIR ONE
ADH : Adriatica
I : I
737 : 733 : 734

AIR OSTRAVA
VTR : Vitek
OK : CZE
SF3

AIR PACIFIC
FJI : Pacific
DQ : FJI
733 : 735 : 738 : 763 : 747

AIR PHILIPPINES
GAP : Orient Pacific
RP : PHL
M80 : YS1 : 73S

AIR PLUS COMET
MPD : Red Comet
EC : E
313

**AIR SCANDIC
INTERNATIONAL**
SCY : Airscann
G : GB
AB4

AIR SEYCHELLES
SEY : Seychelles
S7 : SEY
BNI : DHT : 767 : 763

AIR SICILIA
SIC : Air Sicilia
I : I
AT2 : 73S : 734

AIR SINAI
ASD : Air Sinai
SU : EGY
73S : 735

AIR SOFIA
SFB : Air Sofia
LZ : BUL
AN6 : ANF

AIR TAHITI
VTA : Air Tahiti
F : F-OCE
AT2 : AT4 : AT7 : D28

AIR TAHITI NUI
THT : Tahiti Airlines
F : F-OCE
342

AIR TANZANIA
ATC : Tanzania
5H : TZA
F27 : 73S

AIR TCHAD
HTT : Hotel Tango
TT : TCD
F27

AIR TRANSAT
TSC : Transat
C : CAN
L10 : 332 : 757

AIR TRANSPORT
INTERNATIONAL - ATI
ATN : Air Transport
N : USA
D8F

AIR UKRAINE
UKR : Air Ukraine
UR : UKR
AN4 : AN6 : IL6 : IL 7 : TU3 : TU5

AIR VANUATU
AVN : Air Van
YJ : VUT
EMB : 734

AIR ZIMBABWE
AZW : Zimbabwe
Z : ZWE
146 : 707 : 73S : 767

AIR - INDIA
AIC : Airindia
VT : IND
AB3 : 313 : 747 : 743 : 744

AIRBC
ABL : Aircoach
C : CAN
DH8 : 146

AIRBORNE EXPRESS
ABX : Abex
N : USA
D8F : D9F : DC9 : 767

AIRCALIN - AIR CALEDONIE INTERNATIONAL
ACI : Aircalin
F : F - NCL
DHT : 733

AIRES
ARE : Aires
HK : CLM
EMB : DH8 : F27

AIRFAST INDONESIA
AFE : Airfast
PK : INS
73M : 73S : HS7 : CS2 : DHT : DC3

AIR GEORGIA
GEO : Air Georgia
4L : GEO
TU5

AIRSTAN
JSC : Airstan
RA : RUS
AN6 : IL7 : YK4

**AIRTOURS
INTERNATIONAL**
AIH :Kestrel
G : GB
32S : 321 : 332 : 757 : 763

AIRTRAN
MTE : Citrus
N : USA
DC9 : 73S : 717

AJT AIR
INTERNATIONAL
TRJ : Turjet
RA : RUS
ILW

ALASKA AIRLINES
ASA : Alaska
N : USA
M80 : 73S : 734 : 737

ALBANIAN AIRLINES
LBC : Albanian
ZA : ALB
TU3

ALITALIA
AZA : Alitalia
I : I
AB4 : M80 : M11 : 32S : 321 :
747 : 763

ALL NIPPON AIRWAYS
ANA : All Nippon
JA : J
32S : 321 : 747 : 744 : 767 : 763 :
777

ALLEGRO AIR
GRO : Allegro
XA : MEX
DC9 : M80 : 727

ALOHA AIRLINES
AAH : Aloha
N : USA
73S : 737

ALPI EAGLES
ELG : Alpi Eagles
I : I
100

AMC AVIATION
AMV : AMC
SU : EGY
AB3 : M90 : 73S

AMERER AIR
AMK : Amerer Air
OE : AUT
F27 : LOF

AMERICAN AIRLINES
AAL : American
N : USA
AB3 : D10 : M11 : M80 : 100 :
72S : 738 : 757 : 767 : 763 : 777

AMERICAN EAGLE
EGF : Eagle Flight
N : USA
SF3 : ATR4 : AT7 : EM4

Phoenix Suns

Teamwork

Arizona

Nevada

Ohio

Phoenix Suns

AZ Diamondbacks

AZ Cardinals

AMERICA WEST AIRLINES
AWE : Cactus

N : USA
319 : 32S : 73S : 733 : 757

AMERIJET INTERNATIONAL
AJT : Amerijet
N : USA
72F

ANGOLA AIRCHARTER
AGO : Angola Charter
D2 : AGL
LOH : 73S : 72F : 72M : 70F

ANSETT AUSTRALIA
AAA : Ansett
VH : AUS
F28 : 146 : 32S : 733 : 743 : 767 :
763

ANTONOV AIRLINES
ADB : Antonov
UR : UKR
AN4 : AN6 : ANF : A4F

AOM - FRENCH AIRLINE
AOM : French Lines
F : F
M80 : D10 : 735 : 342

ARIANA AFGHAN AIRLINES
AFG : Ariana
YA : AFG
AN4 : AN6 : TU5 : YK4 : 727

ARKIA ISRAEL
AIZ : Arkia
4X : ISR
AT7 : 73S : 757 : 753

ARMENIAN AIRLINES
RME : Armenian
EK : ARM
ILW : TU3 : TU5 : YK4

ARROW AIR
APW : Big A
N : USA
D8F : L1F

**ASA - ATLANTIC
SOUTHEAST AIRLINES**
ASE : ASEA
N : USA
AT7 : CRJ : EMB

**ASA - AFRICAN SAFARI
AIRWAYS**
QSC : Zebra
5Y : KEN
D10

ASERCA AIRLINES
OCA : Aserca
YV : VEN
DC9 : M90

ASIANA AIRLINES
AAR : Asiana
HL : KOR
321 : 734 : 735 : 763 : 744 : 74F

ASIAN SPIRIT
RIT : Asian Spirit
RP : PHL
DH7 : L4T : YS1

ATA
AMT : Amtran
N : USA
L10 : 72S : 757

ATI AIRCOMPANY
TII : Airati
UR : UKR
IL7

ATLANT - SOYUZ AIRLINES
AYZ : Atlantsoyuz
RA : RUS
ANF : IL8 : IL6 : IL7 : TU3 : TU5

ATLANTIC AIRLINES
AAG : Atlantic
G : GB
DC3 : DC6 : LOF : BNI : SWM

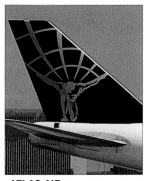

ATLAS AIR
GTI : Giant
N : USA
74F

AUGSBURG AIRWAYS
AUB : Augsburg Air
D : D
DH8

AURIGNY AIRSERVICE
AUR : Ayline
G : GB
BNT : SH6 : SF3

AUSTRIAN AIRLINES
AUA : Austrian
OE : AUT
F70 : M80 : M87 : 313 :
32S : 321 : 332 : 340 : 343

AUSTRALIAN AIR EXPRESS
XME : —
VH : AUS
146 : 72F : SWM

AVANT
VAT : Avant Airlines
CC : CHL
73S

AVENSA
AVE : Ave
YV : VEN
DC9 : D10 : 727 : 72S

AVIACSA
CHP : Aviacsa
XA : MEX
DC9 : 72S

AVIAENERGO
ERG : Aviaenergo
RA : RUS
AN7 : TU3 : TU5 : IL6

AVIANCA COLOMBIA
AVA : Avianca
HK : CLM
F50 : M80 : 72S : 757 : 763

AVIATECA GUATEMALA
GUG : Aviateca
TG : GTM
73S

AVIOGENEX
AGX : Genex
YU : YUG
73S : 72S

AVIOIMPEX
AXX : Avioimpex
Z3 : MKD
DC9 : M80 : YK2

AZERBAIJAN AIRLINES
AHY : Azal
4K : AZE
TU3 : TU5 : YK4 : 72S : 757

AZZURRAAIR
AZI : Azzurra
I : I
ARJ : 737

BAHAMASAIR
BHS : Bahamas
C6 : BAH
DH8 : SH6 : 73S

BAIKAL AIRLINES
BKL : Baikal
RA : RUS
AN4 : AN6 : ANF : IL7 : TU5

BALAIR
BBB : Balair
HB : SUI
763 : 757

BAL - BASHKIRSKIE AVIALINII
BTC : Bashkirian
RA : RUS
AN4 : TU3 : TU5

BALKAN - BULGARIAN AIRLINES
LAZ : Balkan
LZ : BUL
AN4 : ANF : IL8 : TU5 : 735

BANGKOK AIR
BKP : Bangkok Air
HS : THA
AT2 : AT7

BAX GLOBAL
BAX : Global
N : USA
D8F : 72F

BELAIR
BLI : Air Belorus
EW : BLR
IL7 : TU3

BELAVIA
BRU : Belarus Avia
EW : BLR
AN4 : AN6 : TU3 : TU5 : YK4

BELLVIEW
BLV : Bellview Airlines
5N : NIG
DC9 : AB6

**BIMAN BANGLADESH
AIRLINES**
BBC : Bangladesh
S2 : BGD
F28 : D10 : 310

BINTER CANARIAS
IBB : Canaria
EC : E
AT7 : DC9

BLUE PANORAMA
BPA : Blue Jet
I : I
733 : 734

BOURAQ INDONESIA
BOU : Bouraq
PK : INS
HS7 : 73S

BRAATHENS
BRA : Braathens
LN : NOR
734 : 735 : 73G

BRAATHENS MALMÖ AVIATION
SCW : Scanwings
SE : S
100 : 146 : 733 : 735

BRIT AIR
BZH : Britair
F : F
AT2 : AT7 : CRJ

BRITANNIA AIRWAYS
BAL : Britannia
G : GB
738 : 757 : 767 : 763

BRITISH AIRWAYS
BAW : Speedbird
G : GB
SSC : 319 : 32S : 73S : 734 : 735
747 : 744 : 757 : 763 : 777

BRITISH MIDLAND
BMA : Midland
G : GB
EM4 : F70 : SF3 : 100 : 320 : 321 :
733 : 734 : 735

BRITISH WORLD AIRWAYS
BWL : Britworld
G : GB
AT7 : ATP : B11 : 733

BUDDHA AIR
— : Buddhaair
9N : NPL
BE1

BUFFALO AIRWAYS
BFL : Buffalo
C : CAN
CWC : DC3 : DC4

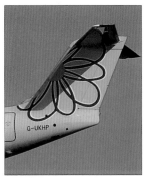

BUZZ
— : —
G : GB
146

BWIA INTERNATIONAL
BWA : West Indian
9Y : TRD
L15 : M80 : 738

CAMEROON AIRLINES
UYC : Camair
TJ : CME
HS7 : 73S : 733 : 747

CANADA 3000 AIRLINES
CMM : Elite
C : CAN
32S : 330 : 757

CANADIAN
CDN : Canadian
C : CAN
D10 : 32S : 73S : 744 : 763

CARGO LION
TLX : Translux
LX : LUX
D8F : D1F

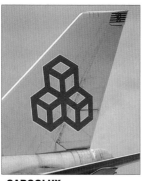

CARGOLUX
CLX : Cargolux
LX : LUX
74F

CASINO EXPRESS
CXP : Casino Express
N : USA
73S

CATA LINEA AEREA
CTZ : Cata
LV : ARG
FK7

CATHAY PACIFIC
CPA : Cathay
B-H : HKG
333 : 343 : 747 : 74F : 744 : 777

CAYMAN AIRWAYS
CAY : Cayman
VP-C : CYM
73S

CEBU PACIFIC
CPI : Cebu Air
RP : PHL
DC9

CHALLENGE AIR CARGO - CAC
CWC : Challenge Cargo
N : USA
D1F

CHAMPION AIR
CCP : Champion Air
N : USA
72S

CHANNEL EXPRESS AIR SERVICE
EXS : Channex
G : GB
ABF : F27 : LOF

CHICAGO EXPRESS AIRLINES
WDY : Windcity
N : USA
J31 : SF3

CHINA AIRLINES
CAL : Cal
B : TWN
AB3 : 738 : 74F : 744

CHINA EASTERN AIRLINES
CES : China Eastern
B : CHN
AB6 : AN4 : M80 : M90 : M1F :
M11 : YN7 : YK2 : 32S : 340 : 733

**CHINA NATIONAL
AVIATION CORP. - CNAC**
CAG : China National
B : CHN
DH8 : 32S

CHINA NORTHERN AIRLINES
CBF : China Northern
B : CHN
AB3 : M80 : M90 : YN7

CHINA NORTHWEST AIRLINES
CNW : China Northwest
B : CHN
AB6 : TU5 : YN5 : YN7 : 146 :
310 : 32S

CHINA SOUTHERN AIRLINES
CSN : China Southern
B : CHN
32S : 733 : 735 : 757 : 777

CHINA SOUTHWEST AIRLINES
CXN : China Southwest
B : CHN
TU5 : YN2 : 733 : 738 : 757 : 340

CHINA UNITED AIRLINES
CUA : Lianhan
B : CHN
AN4 : IL7 : TU5 : 733

CHINA XINHUA AIRLINES
CHX : Xinhua
B : CHN
733 : 734

CHINA XINGJIANG AIRLINES
CXJ : Xinjiang
B : CHN
AT7 : ILW : TU5 : 733 : 757

CHINA YUNNAN AIRLINES
CYH : Yunnan
B : CHN
733 : 738 : 763

CIMBER AIR
CIM : Cimber
OY : DNK
AT2 : AT7

CIRRUS AIRLINES
RUS : Cirrus Air
D : D
DH8 : EM4

CITY BIRD
CTB : Dream Bird
OO : BEL
ABF : M11 : 763 : 74F

CITY JET
BCY : City-Ireland
EI : IRL
146 : S20

COMAIR
COM : Comair
N : USA
CRJ : EM2

COMAIR
CAW : Commercial
ZS : AFS
73S : 72S

**COMPAGNIE CORSE
MEDITERRANEE**
CCM : Corsica
F : F
AT7 : 100

CONDOR
CFG : Condor
D : D
757 : 753 : 763

CONTINENTAL AIRLINES
CON : Continental
N : USA
DC9 : D10 : M80 : 72S : 73S :
733 : 735 : 737 : 738 : 757 : 767 :
764 : 777

COPA PANAMA
CMP : Copa
HP : PNR
73S : 73F : 737

CORSAIR
CRL : Corsair
F : F
330 : 734 : 741 : 743 : 747

CROATIA AIRLINES
CTN : Croatia
9A : HRV
AT2 : 319 : 32S : 73S

CRONUS AIRLINES
CUS : Cronus
SX : GRC
733 : 734

CROSSAIR
CRX : Crossair
HB : SUI
ARJ : EM4 : M80 : SF3 : S20

CSA - CZECH AIRLINES
CSA : CSA-Lines
OK : CZE
AT2 : AT7 : TU5 : 313 : 734 : 735

CUBANA DE AVIACION
CUB : Cubana
CU : CUB
AN4 : AN6 : F27 : IL6 : IL7 : TU5 :
YK2 : 32S

CYPRUS AIRWAYS
CYP : Cyprus
5B : CYP
310 : 32S

DAALLO
DAO : Daloairlines
J2 : DJI
AN4 : TU5

DAS AIR CARGO
DSR : Dasair
5X : UGA
D1F : 70F

DELTA AIR LINES
DAL : Delta
N : USA
L10 : L15 : M80 : M90 : M11 : 72S :
73S : 733 : 738 : 757 : 767 : 764 :
777

DENIM AIR
DNM : Denim
PH : HOL
F50

DEUTSCHE BA
BAG : Speedway
D : D
733

DHL AIRWAYS
DHL : Dahl
N : USA
72F : D8F : AB4

DINAR LINEAS AEREAS
RDN : Aero Dinar
LV : ARG
DC9 : M80

DOMODEDOVO AIRLINES
DMO : Domodedovo
RA : RUS
IL6 : IL7 : IL9

DONAVIA
DNV : Donavia
RA : RUS
ANF : TU3 : TU5

DRAGONAIR
HDA : Loongair
B-H : HKG
32S : 321 : 333

DRUK AIR
DRK : Royal Bhutan
A5 : BTN
146

EAGLE AIR
EGJ : Eagle Jet
N : USA
F27

EAST LINE AIRLINES
ESL : Eastline Express
RA : RUS
ANF : IL6 : IL7 : ILW : TU5

EASY JET AIRLINE
EZY : Easyjet
G : GB
733

ECUATORIANA
EEA : Ecuatoriana
HC : EQA
D10 : 310 : 72S

EDELWEISS AIR
EDW : Edelweiss
HB : SUI
32S

EGYPT AIR
MSR : Egyptair
SU : EGY
AB3 : AB6 : 32S : 321 : 340 :
73S : 735 : 743 : 763 : 777

EL AL ISRAEL AIRLINES
ELY : El Al
4X : ISR
73S : 737 : 738 : 747 : 744 : 74F :
757 : 767

EMERALD AIRWAYS
JEM : Gemstone
G : GB
HS7

EMERY WORLDWIDE
EWW : Emery
N : USA
72F : D8F

EMIRATES
UAE : Emirates
A6 : UAE
AB6 : 313 : 330 : 340 : 777

ENIMEX
ENI : Enimex
ES : EST
AN7

**ERA - EUROPEAN REGIONS
AIRLINES**
EUA : Golden Angel
EC : E
EM4

ERA AVIATION
ERH : Erah
N : USA
DHT : DH8 : CVF

ESTONIAN AIR
ELL : Estonian
ES : EST
F50 : SF3 : 735

ETHIOPIAN AIRLINES
ETH : Ethiopian
ET : ETH
AT4 : DHT : F50 : LOH : 707 :
73S : 757 : 763 : 767

EURALAIR INTERNATIONAL
EUL : Euralair
F : F
73S : 735 : 738

EUROCYPRIA AIRLINES
ECA : Eurocypria
5B : CYP
32S

EUROLOT
ELO : Eurolot
SP : POL
AT2

EUROWINGS
EWG : Eurowings
D : D
AT2 : AT4 : AT7 : 146 : 319

EVA AIR
EVA : Evaair
B : TWN
M11 : M1F : 744 : 767

EVERGREEN INTERNATIONAL
EIA : Evergreen
N : USA
DC9 : 747

EXPRESS ONE
LHN : Longhorn
N : USA
DC9 : 72S

FALCON AVIATION
FCN : Falcon
SE : S
737

**FAR EASTERN AIR
TRANSPORT - FAT**
FEA : —
B : TWN
M80 : 73S : 757

FARNAIR EUROPE
FAT : Farner
HB : SUI
F27

FAST AIR CARRIER
FST : Faster
CC : CHL
D8F

FEDEX
FDX : Fedex
N : USA
ABF : CNA : F27 : D1F : M1F :
SH6 : 312 : 72F

FINE AIR
FBF : Fine Air
N : USA
D8F : L1F

FINNAIR
FIN : Finnair
OH : FIN
AT7 : DC9 : M87 : M11: SF3 :
319 : 320 : 321 : 757

FIRST AIR
FAB : First
C : CAN
DHP : DHT : DH7 : HS7 : 72F :
72M : 73S

FISCHER AIR
FFR : Fischer
OK : CZE
733

FLIGHT WEST AIRLINES
FWQ : —
VH : AUS
J31 : EM2 : F28 : 100

FLUGEFLAG ISLANDS
FXI : Faxi
TF : ISL
DHT : SWM : F50

FLY FTI
FTI : Frogline
D : D
32S

**FREEDOM AIR
INTERNATIONAL**
FOM : Freeair
ZK : NZL
733

**FUTURA INTERNATIONAL
AIRWAYS**
FUA : Futura
EC : E
734 : 738

GANDALF
GAN : Gandalf
I : I
D38

FRONTIER AIRLINES   N : USA
FFT : Frontierflight   73S : 733

GALAXY
— : Galaxy
SX : GRC
733

GARUDA INDONESIA
GIA : Indonesia
PK : INS
AB3 : D10 : 333 : 733 : 734 :
735 : 747 : 744

GAZPROMAVIA
GZP : Gazprom
RA : RUS
AN7 : IL7 : TU3 : TU5 : YK2 : YK4

GEMINI AIR CARGO
LLC : Gemini
N : USA
D1F

GERMANIA
GMI : Germania
D : D
733 : 73G

GHANA AIRWAYS
GHA : Ghana
9G : GHA
F27 : DC9 : D10

GILL AIRWAYS
GIL : Gillair
G : GB
AT2 : AT7 : SH6 : 100

GO FLY
GOE : Go Flight
G : GB
733

GRANDAIR
GDI : Dante Santos
RP : PHL
73S

GROENLANDSFLY
GRL : Greenlandair
OY : DNK
DH7 : DHT : 757

GULF AIR
GFA : Gulfair
A40 : OMA
32S : 333 : 343 : 763

**GULFSTREAM
INTERNATIONAL**
GTF : Gulf Flight
N : USA
BE1 : DH7

HAINAN AIR
CHH : Hainan
B : CHN
SWM : 733 : 734 : 738

**HAMBURG
INTERNATIONAL**
HHI : Lobster
D : D
737

HAPAG - LLOYD
HLF : Hapaglloyd
D : D
310 : 313 : 734 : 735 : 738

HARLEQUIN
HLQ : Harlequin
JA : J
D10 : M80

HAWAIIAN AIR
HAL : Hawaiian
N : USA
DC9 : D10

HAZELTON AIRLINES
HZL : Hazelton
VH : AUS
SWM : SF3

HEAVYLIFT CARGO AIRLINES
HLA : Heavylift
G : GB
ABF : ANF : IL7 : SHB

HELENAIR
HCL : Helencorp
J6 : LCA
DHT : BE1

HEMUS AIR
HMS : Hemus Air
LZ : BUL
L4T : TU3 : YK4

**HINDUJA LUFTHANSA
CARGO SERVICES**
LCI : Lufthansa India
VT : IND
72F

**HOKKAIDO INTERNATIONAL
AIRLINES**
ADO : Air Do
JA : J
763

HORIZON AIR
QXE : Horizonair
N : USA
DH8 : F28

IBERIA
IBE : Iberia
EC : E
AB3 : DC9 : D10 : M87 : D8F : 319
32S : 321 : 343 : 72S : 747 : 757

IBERWORLD
IWD : Iberworld
EC : E
32S : 310

ICELANDAIR
ICE : Iceair
TF : ISL
F50 : 734 : 757

IMPULSE AIRLINES
— : Impulse
VH : AUS
BE1

INDIAN AIRLINES
IAC : Indair
VT : IND
AB3 : D28 : 32S : 73S

INTER AIR
ILN : Inline
ZS : AFS
72S : 707

INVERSIA
INV : Inver
YL : LVA
IL7

IRAN AIR
IRA : Iranair
EP : IRN
AB2 : AB6 : 100 : 707 : 70F :
727 : 73S : 74L : 74F : 747

IRAN ASSEMAN AIRLINES
IRC : —
EP : IRN
AT2 : AT7 : BNI : F28 : 72S

ISLANDSFLUG
ICB : Icebird
TF : ISL
AT2 : D28 : SWM : 73S

ISLENA AIRLINES
ISV : Islena
HR : HND
AT2 : L4T : SH6

ISRAIR
ISR : Israir
4X : ISR
AT2 : 73S

ISTANBUL AIRLINES
IST : Istanbul
TC : TUR
733 : 734 : 738

ITALAIR
DRG : Italair
I : I
AT2

JAL EXPRESS
JEX : Janex
JA : J
734

JANA ARKA
JAK : Yanzar
UN : KAZ
TU5

JAPAN AIR COMMUTER
JAC : Commuter
JA : J
SF3 : YS1

JAPAN AIRLINES
JAL : Japanair
JA : J
D10 : M11 : 734 : 74F : 747 :
743 : 744 : 763 : 777

JAPAN AIR SYSTEM
JAS : Airsystem
JA : J
AB2 : AB3 : AB6 : M80 : M87 :
M90 : D10 : 777

JAPAN ASIA AIRWAYS
JAA : Asia
JA : J
D10 : 747 : 743

JAPAN TRANSOCEAN AIR
JTA : Jai Ocean
JA : J
DHT : YS1 : 73S : 734

JARO INTERNATIONAL
MDJ : Jaro International
YR : ROU
B11 : 707

JAT - YUGOSLAV AIRLINES
JAT : JAT
YU : YUG
AT7 : DC9 : D10 : 72S : 733

JERSEY EUROPEAN AIRWAYS
JEA : Jersey
G : GB
F27 : SH6 : DH8 : 146

JET AIRWAYS
JAI : Jet Airways
VT : IND
733 : 734

JETBLUE
— : —
N : USA
32S

JETCRAFT AVIATION
— : Jetcraft
VH : AUS
SWM : DH7 : J41

JMC
JMC : Jay-emm-cee
G : GB
32S : 757 : D1C

KALININGRAD AVIA
KLN : Kaliningrad Air
RA : RUS
TU3 : TU5

KARAT
AKT : Aviakarat
RA : RUS
AN4 : YK2

KELOWNA FLIGHTCRAFT
KFA : Flightcraft
C : CAN
CNA : CVF : CVR : 727

KENYA AIRWAYS
KQA : Kenya
5Y : KEN
F50 : 313 : 73S : 733

KHALIFA
— : —
7T : ALG
32S : 310 : 734

KISH AIR
IRK : Kishair
EP : IRN
TU5 : YK4

KITTY HAWK AIR CARGO
KHA : Air Kittihawk
N : USA
CVF : D9F : 72F

KITTY HAWK INTERNATIONAL
CKS : Connie
N : USA
D8F : L1F : 74F : 747

KLM CITYHOPPER
KLC : City
PH : HOL
F50 : F70

KLM EXEL
AXL : Exel Commuter
PH : HOL
AT2 : AT7 : EM2

KLM - ROYAL DUTCH AIRLINES
KLM : KLM
PH : HOL
M11 : 733 : 734 : 738 : 747 : 743 :
744 : 763

KLM UK
UKA : Ukay
G : GB
AT7 : F50 : 100 : 146

**KMV - KAVKAZSKIE
MINERALNYE VODY**
MVD : Air Minvody
RA : RUS
TU3 : TU5 : T20

KOLAVIA
KGL : Kogalym
RA : RUS
TU3 : TU5

KOREAN AIR
KAL : Koreanair
HL : KOR
ABF : AB3 : AB6 : M80 : M11 :
100 : 332 : 333 : 737 : 747 : 743 :
747 : 74F : 777

KOSMOS AVIAKOMPANIA
KSM : Kosmos
RA: RUS
AN6 : ANF : IL7 : TU3

KTHY - KIBRIS TÜRK HAVA YOLLARI
KYV : Airkibris
TC : N-CYP
310 : 72S : 738

KRAS AIR
KJC : Krasnoyorsky
RA : RUS
AN4 : IL6 : IL7 : ILW : TU5 : YK4

KUBAN AIRLINES
KIL : Air Kuban
RA : RUS
AN4 : AN6 : YK2

KUWAIT AIRWAYS
KAC : Kuwaiti
9K : KWT
AB6 : 313 : 343 : 32S : 747 : 744

KYRGHYZSTAN AIRLINES
KGA : Kyrgyz
EX : KGZ
AN6 : IL7 : TU5: YK4

L'AEROPOSTALE
ARP : Aeroposte
F : F
AB4 : 72F : 73F : 733

LAB - LLOYD AEREO BOLIVIANO
LLB : Lloyd Aereo
CP : BOL
F27 : 313 : 70F : 72S : 733

LACSA COSTA RICA
LRC : Lacsa
TI : CTR
73S : 32S

LADECO AIRLINES
LCO : Ladeco
CC : CHL
73S

LAER - LINEAS AEREAS ENTRE RIOS
— : —
LV : ARG
J31 : AT2

LAKER AIRWAYS
LKR : Laker
N : USA
727

LAM - LINHAS AEREAS DE MOCAMBIQUE
LAM : Mozambique
C9 : MOZ
CS2 : 100 : 73S : 767

LAN CHILE
LAN : Lan
CC : CHL
73S : 763

LAO AVIATION
LAO : Lao
RDPL : LAO
AN4 : AT7 : YN7 : YN2 : YK4

**LAPA - LINEAS AEREAS
PRIVADAS ARGENTINAS**
LPR : Lapa
LV : ARG
73S : 73G : 757

LAUDA AIR
LDA : Laudaair
OE : AUT
CRJ : 733 : 734 : 736 :763 : 777

LAUDA AIR ITALY
LDI : Lauda Italy
I : I
767 : CRJ

**LGW - LUFTFAHRT-
GESELLSCHAFT WALTER**
LGW : Walter
D : D
D28

LIAT
LIA : Liat
V2 : ATG
BNI : DHT : DH8

LIBYAN ARAB AIRLINES
LAA : Libair
5A : LBY
F28 : 72S : 32S

**LINEAS AEREAS
SURAMERICAS**
LAU : Suramericano
HK : CLM
CRV : 72F

LITHUANIAN AIRLINES
LIL : Lithuania Air
LY : LTU
SF3 : S20 : YK2 : 73S

LOGANAIR
LOG : Logan
G : GB
BNI : DHT : SH6

**LOT - POLSKIE LINIE
LOTNICZE**
LOT : Lot
SP : POL
AT7 : EM4 : 733 : 734 : 735 : 767 :
763

LOTUS AIR
TAS : Lotus Flower
SU :EGY
32S

**LTU INTERNATIONAL
AIRWAYS**
LTU : LTU
D : D
32S : 757 : 763 : 333

LUFTHANSA
DLH : Lufthansa
D : D
AB6 : 313 : 319 : 32S : 321 : 340 :
343 : 733 : 735 : 74M : 747 : 744

LUFTHANSA CITYLINE
CLH : Hansaline
D : D
ARJ : CRJ

LUXAIR
LGL : Luxair
LX : LUX
EM4 : F50 : 734 : 735

LYNDEN AIR CARGO
LYC : Lynden
N : USA
LOH

MAERSK AIR
DAN : Maerskair
OY : DNK
F50 : 733 : 735 : 73G

MAHFOOZ AVIATION
MZS : Mahfooz
C5 : GMB
707 : 72S

MALAYSIA AIRLINES
MAS : Malaysian
9M : MLA
DHT : F50 : 333 : 734 : 735 :
744 : 777

**MALEV HUNGARIAN
AIRLINES**
MAH : Malev
HA : HNG
F70 : TU5 : 73S : 733 : 734

MANDALA AIRLINES
MDL : Mandala
PK : INS
F28 : 73S

MANDARIN AIRLINES
MDA : Mandarin Air
B : TWN
M11 : D28 : F50 : 100

MANX
MNX : Manx
G : GB
ATP : 146

MARTINAIR
MPH : Martinair
PH : HOL
EM2 : M11 : M1M : 747 : 74F : 763

MAT - MACEDONIAN AIRLINES
MAK : Makavio
Z3 : MKD
DC9 : 733

MEA - MIDDLE EAST AIRLINE
MEA : Cedarjet
OD : LBN
313 : 32S : 321 : 747

MERIDIANA
ISS : Merair
I : I
DC9 : M80 : 146

MERPATI
MNA : Merpati
PK : INS
CS2 : CS5 : DHT : F27 : F28 :
100 : 73S

MESA AIRLINES
ASH : Air Shuttle
N : USA
CRJ : BE1 : DH8

METROJET
MET : —
N : USA
73S

MEXICANA
MXA : Mexicana
XA : MEX
100 : 32S : 72S : 757

MIAMI AIR
BSK : Biscayne
N : USA
72S

MIAT - MONGOLIAN AIRLINES
MGL : Mongolair
JU : MNG
AN4 : AN6 : 727: 310

MIDWAY AIRLINES
MDW : Midway
N : USA
CRJ : 100 : 32S : 737

MIDWEST AIRLINE
— : —
SU : EGY
310

MIDWEST EXPRESS
MEP : Midex
N : USA
DC9 : M80

MK AIRLINES
MKA : —
9G : GHA
D8F : 74F

MNG CARGO AIRLINES
MNB : Black Sea
TC : TUR
AB4

MOLDAVIAN AIRLINES
MDV : Moldavian
ER : MDA
SF3 : TU3 : YK4

MONARCH AIRLINES
MON : Monarch
G : GB
D10 : AB6 : 32S : 321 : 330 : 757

MUK AIR
MUK : Mukair
OY : DNK
AT2 : EMB : J31 : SH6

MYANMA AIRWAYS
UBA : Unionair
XY : BRM
F27 : F28

NATIONAL AIRLINES
ROK : Red Rock
N : USA
757

NATIONAL JET SYSTEM
NJS : National Jet
VH : AUS
ARJ : DH8 : 146

NATIONWIDE AIR
NTW : Nationwide Air
ZS : AFS
B11 : 727 : 72F : 73S

NICA AIRLINES
NIS : Nica
YN : NCG
73S

NIGERIA AIRWAYS
NGA : Nigeria
5N : NIG
D10 : 310 : 73S

NIPPON CARGO AIRLINES
NCA : Nippon Cargo
JA : J
74F

**NORTH AMERICAN
AIRLINES**
NAO : North American
N : USA
738 : 757

NORTHERN AIR CARGO
NAC : Northern Air Cargo
N : USA
D6F : 72F

NORTHWEST AIRLINES
NWA : Northwest
N : USA
DC9 : D10 : M80 : 319 : 32S :
72S : 74F : 747 : 744 : 757

NOUVELAIR TUNESIE
LBT : Nouvelair
TS : TUN
M80 : 32S

NOVAIR
NVR : Navigator
SE : S
L15 : 738

ODESSA AIR
ODS : Odessa Air
UR : UKR
TU5 : YK4

OKADA AIR
OKJ : Okadaair
5N : NIG
B11 : 72S

**OLT - OSTFRIESISCHE
LUFTTRANSPORT**
OLT : Oltra
D : D
BNI : CNA : SF3 : SWM

OLYMPIC AIRWAYS
OAL : Olympic
SX : GRC
AB3 : AB6 : 340 : 73S : 734 :
738 : 747

OLYMPIC AVIATION
OLY : Olavia
SX : GRC
AT2 : AT7 : D28 : 717

OMAN AIR
OMA : Omanair
A4O : OMA
AT4 : DHT : 313

OMNI AIR INTERNATIONAL
OAI : Omni Express
N : USA
D10

ONUR AIR
OHY : Onur Air
TC : TUR
AB3 : M80 : 32S : 321

ORENBURG AIRLINES
ORB : Orenburg
RA : RUS
AN4 : TU3 : TU5

ORIENT THAI AIRLINES
OEA : Orient Express
HS : THA
L10

ORBI AIR COMPANY
DVU : Zena
4L : GEO
TU3

PACIFIC COASTAL
PCO : Pasco
C : CAN
CNA : BE1 : DH2 : BNI : EMB :
SH6

PALESTINIAN AIRLINES
PNW : Palestinian
— : PAL
F50 : 72S

PAN AM
PXA : Clipper
N : USA
727

PANTANAL
PTN : Pantanal
PT-PP : B
AT2 : EM2

**PASSAREDO TRANSPORTES
AEREOS**
PTB : Passaredo
PT-PP : B
AT2 : EM2 : 313

PEGASUS AIRLINES
PGT : Pegasus
TC : TUR
734 : 738

PELITA AIR
PAS : Pelita
PK : INS
ARJ : CS2 : DH7 : F28

PERM AIRLINES
PGP : Perm Air
RA : RUS
AN4 : AN6 : TU3 : TU5 : YK4

PETROLEUM AIR SERVICES
PAS : Petroleum
SU : EGY
DH7

PHILIPPINES
PAL : Philippine
RP : PHL
32S : 333 : 343 : 744

**PIA - PAKISTAN
INTERNATIONAL**
PIA : Pakistan
AP : PAK
AB3 : DHT : F27 : 313: 70F :
733 : 747

PLUNA
PUA : Pluna
CX : URG
73S

POLAR AIR CARGO
PAC : Polar Tiger
N : USA
74F

POLYNESIAN
PAO : Polynesian
5W : SMO
BN1 : DHT : 733

PORTUGALIA AIRLINES
PGA : Portugalia
CS : POR
EM4 : 100

PREMIAIR
VKG : Viking
OY : DNK
AB4 : D10 : 32S : 330

PROAIR
PRH : Prohawk
N : USA
733 : 734

PULKOVO AVIATION
PLK : Pulkovo
RA : RUS
ANF : ILW : TU3 : TU5

QANTAS
QFA : Qantas
VH : AUS
733 : 734 : 747 : 74L : 744 : 767 :
763

QATAR AIRWAYS
QTR : Qatari
A7 : QAT
AB6 : 32S

RAF AVIA
MTL : Mitavia
YL : LVA
AN6

REEVE ALEUTIAN AIRWAYS
RVV : Reeve
N : USA
LOE : YS1 : 72M

REGIONAL AIRLINES
RGI : Regional
F : F
EM3 : EM4 : J31 : SF3 : S20

RHEINTALFLUG
RTL : Rheintal
OE : AUT
DH8 : EM4

RIO SUL
RSL : Riosul
PP-PT : B
EM2 : F50 : 735

ROMAVIA
RMV : Aeromavia
YR : ROU
IL8 : B11 : 707

ROYAL AIR MAROC
RAM : Marocair
CN : MRC
AT2 : 72S : 73S : 734 : 735 :
738 : 747 : 744 : 757

ROYAL AIR CAMBODGE
RAC : Royal Cambodge
XU : —
AT7 : YN2 : 734

ROYAL AVIATION
ROY : Roy
C : CAN
313 : 72S : 73S : 757

ROYAL BRUNEI AIRLINES
RBA : Brunei
V8 : BRU
757 : 763

ROYAL JORDANIAN
RJA : Jordanian
JY : JOR
310 : 313 : 32S : 70F

ROYAL NEPAL AIRLINES
RNA : Royal Nepal
9N : NPL
DHT : HS7 : 757

RYANAIR
RYR : Ryanair
EI : IRL
73S : 738

SA EXPRESS
EXY : Expressways
ZS : AFS
DH8 : CRJ

SABENA
SAB : Sabena
OO : BEL
319 : 320 : 321 : 340 : 343 :
733 : 734 : 735

SABRE AIRWAYS
SBE : Sabre
G : GB
72S : 73S : 738

SAE SWE AVIATION EUROPE
SWL : Swing
SE : S
F27

SAHARA
— : —
VT : IND
73S : 733 : 734

SAM COLOMBIA
SAM : Sam
HK : CLM
ARJ : CNA

SAMARA AIRLINES
BRZ : Beryoza
RA : RUS
ANF : IL7 : TU3 : TU5

SANTA CRUZ IMPERIAL
SNZ : Santa Cruz
EL : LBR
AN4 : AN6 : ANF : IL8 : 70F

SARAVIA
SOV : Saratov Air
RA : RUS
AN4 : YK2

SATA AIR ACORES
SAT : Sata
CS : POR-AZR
ATP : D28 : 733

SATENA
NSE : Satena
HK-FAC : CLM
D28 : D38 : F28 : 72F

SAUDI ARABIAN AIRLINES
SVA : Saudia
HZ : ARS
AB6 : L10 : M11 : M90 : 73S :
747 : 744 : 777

SCANDINAVIAN COMMUTER
SAS : Scandinavian
SE : S*
DH8 : F50 : S20

SCANDINAVIAN - SAS
SAS : Scandinavian
SE : S*
DC9 : M80 : M87 : M90 : 736 :
763

SCENIC AIRLINES
YRR : Scenic
N : USA
BE1 : CNA

SCHREINER AIRWAYS
SCH : Schreiner
PH : HOL
AB3 : DH8

SCOT AIRWAYS
SAY : Scot
G : GB
D28 : D38

SERVIVENSA
SVV : Servivensa
YV : VEN
DC3 : DC9 : 727 : 72S : 73S

SHANDONG AIRLINES
CDG : Shandong
B : CHN
SF3 : 735

SHANGHAI AIRLINES
CSH : Shanghaiair
B : CHN
733 : 73G : 757 : 763

SHENZEN AIRWAYS
CSZ : Shenzen Air
B : CHN
733 : 73G

SHOROUK AIR
SHK : Shorouk
SU : EGY*
32S

SHUTTLE AMERICA
TCF : Shuttlecraft
N : USA
DH8

SIBAVIATRANS
SIB : Sibavia
RA : RUS
AN6 : TU5 : YK4

SIBIR AIRLINES
SBI : Siberia Airlines
RA : RUS
AN4 : AN6 : ILW : TU3 : TU5

SICHUAN AIRLINES
CSC : Chuanghang
B : CHN
TU5 : YN7 : 32S : 321

SILKAIR
SLK : Silkair
9V : SNG
F70 : 733 : 319: 32S

SINGAPORE AIRLINES
SIA : Singapore
9V : SNG
310 : 343 : 747 : 74F : 744 : 777

SKYMARK AIRLINES
SKY : Skymark
JA : J
763

SKYSERVICE
SSV : Skyfinder
C : CAN
32S : 333

SKYTEAM
XST : Skyteam
D : D
F27

SKYWAYS
SKX : Sky Express
SE : S
EM4 : F50 : SF3

SKYWEST AIRLINES
SKW : Skywest
N : USA
EM2 : CRJ

SLOVENSKE AEROLINIE
SLL : Slovline
OM : SVK
SF3 : TU5

SOBELAIR
SLR : Sobelair
OO : BEL
733 : 734 : 763

SOLOMONS
SOL : Solomon
H4 : SLM
BNI : DHT : 733

SOUTH AFRICAN AIRWAYS
SAA : Springbok
ZS : AFS
AB3 : ABF : 32S : 73S : 747 :
74L : 744 : 767

SOUTHWEST AIRLINES
SWA : Southwest
N : USA
73S : 733 : 735 : 73G

SOUTHERN WINDS
SWD : Southern Winds
LV : ARG
DH8 : CRJ

SPAIR AIR TRANSPORT
PAR : Spair
RA : RUS
ANF : IL8 : IL7 : TU5

SPANAIR
SPP : Sunwing
EC : E
M80 : 763

SPIRIT AIRLINES
SWG : Spirit Wings
N : USA
DC9 : M80 : M87

SRILANKAN
SRF : Airlanka
4R : CLN
32S : 330 : 340

STAF CARGO
STU : Fueguino
LV : ARG
M1F

STAR EUROPE
SEU : Starway
F : F
32S : 733

STERLING EUROPEAN AIRLINES
SNB : Sterling
OY : DNK
72S : 738

SUDAN AIRWAYS
SUD : Sudanair
ST : SDN
DHT : AB6 : 707

SUN COUNTRY AIRLINES
SCX : Suncountry
N : USA
72S : D10

SUNEXPRESS
SXS : Sunexpress
TC : TUR*
733 : 734

SUNFLOWER AIRLINES
SUF : Sunflower
DQ : FJI
BNI : DHT: SH6

SURINAM AIRWAYS
SLM : Surinam
PZ : SUR
DHT : M87

SWISSAIR
SWR : Swissair
HB : SUI
M11 : 319 : 32S : 321: 330

SYRIANAIR
SYR : Syrianair
YK : SYR
AN4 : AN6 : IL7 : TU3 : TU5 :
YK4 : 32S : 72S : 74L

TAAG ANGOLA AIRWAYS
DTA : DTA
D2 : AGL
F27 : IL6 : 707 : 73S : 74D

TACA
TAI : Taca
YS : SLV
319 : 32S. 73S : 733 : 767 : 763

**TACV - CABO VERDE
AIRLINES**
TCV : Transverde
D4 : CPV
AT2 : DHT : 757

TAJIKISTAN AIRLINES
TJK : Tajikistan
EY : TJK
AN4 : AN6 : TU3 : TU5 : YK4

TAM
TAM : Tam
PP-PT : B
F27 : F50 : 100 : 319 : 32S : 330

TAME
TAE : Tame
HC : EQA
F28 : HS7 : 727 : 72S

TAMPA COLOMBIA
TPA : Tampa
HK : CLM
70F : D8F

TANS-TRANSPORTES AEREOS NATIONALES DE LA SELVA
ELV : Aereos Selva
OB : PRU
F27 : 73S : DHT : YN2

TAP AIR PORTUGAL
TAP : Air Portugal
CS : POR
319 : 32S : 313 : 343

TAROM
ROT : Tarom
YR : ROU
AN4 : AT4 : B11 : TU5 : 313 :
70F : 733

**THAI AIRWAYS
INTERNATIONAL**
THA : Thai
HS : THA
AT7 : M11 : AB6 : 333 : 734 :
747 : 744 : 777

TITAN AIRWAYS
AWC : Zap
G : GB
AT2 : SH6 : 146 : 733

**TNT INTERNATIONAL
AVIATION SERVICES**
NTR : Nitro
G : GB*
14F : 72F : AB4

TOWER AIR
TOW : Tee Air
N : USA
74F : 747

**TRANSAER INTERNATIONAL
AIRWAYS**
EFF : Translift
EI : IRL
AB3 : 32S

TRANSAERO AIRLINES
TSO : Transaero
RA : RUS
ILW : 73S

TRANSASIA
TNA : Foshing
B : TWN
AT4 : AT7 : 32S : 321

TRANSAVIA AIRLINES
TRA : Transavia
PH : HOL
733 : 738 : 757

TRANSBRASIL
TBA : Transbrasil
PT : B
733 : 734 : 767 : 763

**TRANS CONTINENTAL
AIRLINES**
TCN : Transcon
N : USA
D8F: 72F

TRANSEUROPEAN
TEP : Transeurline
RA : RUS
TU5 : T20

TRANSMERIDIAN AIRLINES
TRZ : Transmeridian
N : USA
72S : 32S

TRANSMILE AIR SERVICES
TSE : Transmile
9M : MLA
CNA : 73F : 73S

TRANSTATE AIRLINES
– : –
VH : AUS
BNI : DHT : EMB

TRANS STATES AIRLINES
LOF : Waterski
N : USA
J31 : J41 : AT4 : AT7 : EM4

**TRANS WORLD
AIRLINES - TWA**
TWA : TWA
N : USA
DC9 : M80 : 717 : 72S : 757 :
767 : 763

TRAVEL SERVICE AIRLINES
TVS : Skytravel
OK : CZE
734 : TU5

**TTA - TRANS TRAVEL
AIRLINES**
TRQ : Hunter
PH : HOL
BE1 : DH8

TULPAR AVIATION COMPANY
TUL : Ursal
RA : RUS
AN6 : YK2 : YK4

TUNINTER
TUI : Tuninter
TS : TUN
AT2 : AT7 : DC9 : 73S

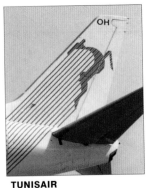

TUNISAIR
TAR : Tunair
TS : TUN
319 : 32S : 72S : 73S : 735 : 736

TURKISH AIRLINES
THY : Turkair
TC : TUR
ARJ : 310 : 313 : 343 : 734 : 738

**TURKMENISTAN/
AKHAL AIRCOMPANY**
AKH : Akhal
EZ : TKM
AN4 : IL7 : TU5 : YK2 : 733 : 757

TYROLEAN AIRWAYS
TYR : Tyrolean
OE : AUT
CRJ : DH8 : F70

TYUMEN AIRLINES
TYM : Air Tyumen
RA : RUS
AN4 : AN6 : ANF : IL7 : TU3 :
TU5

**UKRAINE INTERNATIONAL
AIRLINES**
AUI : Ukraine International
UR : UKR
73S : 733

U-LAND
WIA : —
B : TWA
SH6 : M82

UNITED AIRLINES
UAL : United
N : USA
D10 : 319 : 32S : 72S : 73S :
733 : 735 : 747 : 744 : 757 :
767 : 763 : 777

UPS AIRLINES
UPS : UPS
N : USA
ABF : D8F : 72F : 747 : 75F :
76F

URAL AIRLINES
SVR : Sverdlovsk Air
RA : RUS
AN4 : ANF : ILW : TU5

US AIRWAYS
USA : US Air
N : USA
DC9 : M80 : 100 : 319 : 320 :
330 : 73S : 733 : 734 : 757 : 767

USA JET AIRLINES
JUS : Jet USA
N : USA
D9F

UZBEKISTAN AIRWAYS
UZB : Uzbek
UK : UZB
AN4 : IL4 : IL6 : IL7 : ILW : TU5 :
YK4 : 313 : 763

VANGUARD AIRLINES
VGD : Vanguard Air
N : USA
73S

VARIG
VRG : Varig
PP : B
D10 : M11 : 727 : 73S : 733 :
738 : 743 : 767 : 763

VASP
VASP : Vasp
PP : B
M11 : AB2 : 72S : 73S : 733

VIA EST VITA
VIM : Via
LZ : BUL
TU5

VIETNAM AIRLINES
HVN : Vietnam Airlines
VN : VTN
AT7 : F70 : IL8 : TU3 : 32S : 763

VIPAIR AIRLINES
VPA : Viair
UN : KAZ
TU5

VIRGIN ATLANTIC
VIR : Virgin
G : GB
32S : 343 : 747 : 744

VIRGIN EXPRESS
EBA : Belstar
OO : BEL
733 : 734

VIRGIN SUN
— : —
G : GB
32S

**VLM VLAAMSE
LUCHTTRANSPORT**
VLM : Rubens
OO : BEL
F50

VNUKOVO AIRLINES
VKO : Vnukovo
RA : RUS
ILW : TU5 : T20 : YK2

VOLARE AIRLINES
CDF : Revola
I : I
32S

VOLGA DNEPR AIRLINES
VDA : Volga Dnepr
RA : RUS
A4F : IL7 : IL9 : YK4

WESTJET AIRLINES
— : West Jet
C : CAN
73S

WDL AVIATION
WDL : WDL
D : D
F27 : 146

WIDEROE
WIF : Wideroe
LN : NOR
DHT : DH8

WORLD AIRWAYS
WOA : World
N : USA
D10 : D1F : M11 : M1F

WUHAN AIR LINES
CWU : Wuhan Air
B : CHN
YN7 : 733

XIAMEN AIRLINES
CXA : Xiamen
B : CHN
73S : 735 : 757

YEMENIA
IYE : Yemeni
7O : YEM
DHT : DH7 : 313 : 72S : 73S : LOH

ZHONGYUAN AIRLINES
CYN : Zhongyuan
B : CHN
YN7 : 733

Country codes / abbreviations

e.g.: 3B   = Aircraft national registration prefix
     MAU = ITU (International Telecom Union) - abbreviation
     *   = Multinational

3A	MCO	Monaco	9M	MLA	Malaysia
3B	MAU	Mauritius	9N	NPL	Nepal
3C	GNE	Equatorial Guinea	9Q	ZAI	Congo (ex Zaire)
3D	SWZ	Swaziland	9U	BDI	Burundi
3X	GUI	Guinea	9V	SNG	Singapore
4K	AZE	Azerbaijan	9XR	RRW	Rwanda
4L	GEO	Georgia	9Y	TRD	Trinidad/Tobago
4R	CLN	Sri Lanka	A2	BOT	Botswana
4X	ISR	Israel	A3	TON	Tonga
5A	LBY	Libya	A4O	OMA	Oman
5B	CYP	Cyprus	A5	BTN	Bhutan
5H	TZA	Tanzania	A6	UAE	United Arab Emirates
5N	NIG	Nigeria	A7	QAT	Qatar
5R	MDG	Madagascar	A9C	BHR	Bahrain
5T	MTN	Mauretania	AP	PAK	Pakistan
5U	NGR	Niger	B	CHN	Peoples Republic of China
5V	TGO	Togo			
5W	SMO	Western Samoa	B	TWN	Taiwan
5X	UGA	Uganda	B-H	HKG	Hong Kong
5Y	KEN	Kenya	B-M	MAC	Macau
6O	SOM	Somalia	C	CAN	Canada
6V	SEN	Senegal	C2	NRU	Nauru
6Y	JMC	Jamaica	C3	AND	Andorra
7O	YEM	Yemen	C5	GMB	Gambia
7P	LSO	Lesotho	C6	BAH	Bahamas
7Q	MWI	Malawi	C9	MOZ	Mozambique
7T	ALG	Algeria	CC	CHL	Chile
8P	BRB	Barbados	CF	CAN	Canada (old)
8Q	MLD	Maldives	CN	MRC	Morocco
8R	GUY	Guyana	CP	BOL	Bolivia
9A	HRV	Croatia	CS	POR	Portugal
9G	GHA	Ghana	–	AZR	P-Azores
9H	MLT	Malta	CU	CUB	Cuba
9J	ZMB	Zambia	CX	URG	Uruguay
9K	KWT	Kuwait	D	D	Germany
9L	SRL	Sierra Leone	D2	AGL	Angola

D4	CPV	Cape Verde	JA	J	Japan
D6	COM	Comores	JU	MNG	Mongolia
DQ	FJI	Fiji	JY	JOR	Jordan
E3	ERI	Eritrea	LN	NOR	Norway
EC	E	Spain	–	SVB	Spitzbergen
EI	IRL	Ireland	LV	ARG	Argentina
EK	ARM	Armenia	LX	LUX	Luxembourg
EL	LBR	Liberia	LY	LTU	Lithuania
EP	IRN	Iran	LZ	BUL	Bulgaria
ER	MDA	Moldavia	N	USA	United States
ES	EST	Estonia			of America
ET	ETH	Ethiopia	–	GUM	Guam
EW	BLR	Belarus	–	PTR	Puerto Rico
EX	KGZ	Kyrgystan	–	SMA	American Samoa
EY	TJK	Tajikistan	–	VIR	American Virgin Islands
EZ	TKM	Turkmenistan	OB	PRU	Peru
F	F	France	OD	LBN	Lebanon
–	GUF	French Guyana	OE	AUT	Austria
–	OCE	French Polynesia	OH	FIN	Finland
–	GDL	Guadeloupe	OK	CZE	Czech Republic
–	MRT	Martinique	OM	SVK	Slovakia
–	NCL	New Caledonia	OO	BEL	Belgium
–	REU	Reunion	OY	DNK	Denmark
G	GB	Great Britain	–	FAR	Faroe Islands
H4	SLM	Solomon Islands	P	KRE	Peoples Republic
HA	HNG	Hungary			of Korea
HB	SUI	Switzerland	P2	PNG	Papua-New Guinea
HC	EQA	Ecuador	P4	NA	Aruba
HH	HTI	Haiti	PH	HOL	Netherlands
HI	DOM	Dominican Republic	PJ	ATN	Netherlands Antilles
HK	CLM	Columbia	PK	INS	Indonesia
HL	KOR	Republic of Korea	PP	B	Brazil
HP	PNR	Panama	PT	B	Brazil
HR	HND	Honduras	PZ	SUR	Surinam
HS	THA	Thailand	RA	RUS	Russia
HZ	ARS	Saudi Arabia	RDPL	LAO	Laos
I	I	Italy	RP	PHL	Philippines
J2	DJI	Djibouti	S2	BGD	Bangladesh
J3	GRD	Grenada	S5	SVN	Slovenia
J5	GNB	Guinea-Bissau	S7	SEY	Seychelles
J6	LCA	Saint Lucia	S9	STP	Sao Tome and Principe
J7	DMA	Dominica	SE	S	Sweden
J8	VCT	St Vincent/Grenadines	SP	POL	Poland

ST	SDN	Sudan		VP-A	AIA	Anguilla
SU	EGY	Egypt		VP-B	BER	Bermuda
SX	GRC	Greece		VP-C	CYM	Cayman Islands
T2	TUV	Tuvalu		VP-F	FLK	Falkland Islands
T3	KIR	Kiribati		VP-G	GIB	Gibraltar
T9	BIH	Bosnia-Herzegovina		VP-L	VRG	British Virgin Islands
TC	TUR	Turkey		VP-M	MSR	Montserrat
TF	ISL	Iceland		VQ-T	TCA	Turks and Caicos Islands
TG	GTM	Guatemala				
TI	CTR	Costa Rica		VT	IND	India
TJ	CME	Cameroon		XA-B-C	MEX	Mexico
TL	CAF	Central African Republic		XT	BFA	Burkina Faso
				XU	CBG	Cambodia
TN	COG	Congo		XY	BRM	Myanmar
TR	GAB	Gabon		YA	AFG	Afghanistan
TS	TUN	Tunisia		YI	IRQ	Iraq
TT	TCD	Chad		YJ	VUT	Vanuatu
TU	CTI	Ivory Coast		YK	SYR	Syria
TY	BEN	Benin		YL	LVA	Lithuania
TZ	MLI	Mali		YN	NCG	Nicaragua
UK	UZB	Uzbekistan		YR	ROU	Rumania
UN	KAZ	Kazakhstan		YS	SLV	El Salvador
UR	UKR	Ukraine		YU	YUG	Yugoslavia
V2	ATG	Antigua/Barbuda		–	SER	Serbia
V3	BEL	Belize		YV	VEN	Venezuela
V4	SCN	Saint Kitts/Nevis		Z	ZWE	Zimbabwe
V5	NMB	Namibia		Z3	MKD	Macedonia
V6	–	Micronesia		ZA	ALB	Albania
V7	MRL	Marshall Islands		ZK	NZL	New Zealand
V8	BRU	Brunei		–	CKH	Cook Islands
VH	AUS	Australia		ZP	PRG	Paraguay
VN	VTN	Vietnam		ZS, ZU	AFS	South Africa

We hope you enjoyed this book . . .

Midland Publishing titles are edited
by an experienced and enthusiastic
team of specialists.

Further titles are in preparation
though we welcome ideas from
authors or readers for books they
would like to see published.

In addition, our associate company,
Midland Counties Publications, offers
an exceptionally wide range of
aviation, spaceflight, astronomy,
military, naval and transport books
and videos for sale by mail-order
around the world.

For a copy of the appropriate
catalogue, or to order further copies
of this book, or the titles featured on
the following pages, please write,
telephone, fax or e-mail to:

Midland Counties Publications
Unit 3 Maizefield, Hinckley, Leics.,
LE10 1YF, England
Tel: (+44) 01455 233 747
Fax: (+44) 01455 233 737
E-mail:
midlandbooks@compuserve.com

US distribution by **Specialty Press** -
details on page 2

Softback
240 x 170 mm, 224 pages
252 colour photographs
1 85780 091 5
Published April 2000
UK £14.95 / US $24.95

AIRLINES REMEMBERED

B I Hengi

In the same format as the enormously popular *Airlines Worldwide* and *Airliners Worldwide,* this new companion volume reviews the histories and operations of over 200 airlines from the last 30 years of aviation history, which are no longer with us.

Each is illustrated with a full colour photo showing at least one of their aircraft in the colour scheme of that era. Operators such as BEA, CP Air, Eastern, Jet 24, Laker , Fred Olsen, PeoplExpress and Valujet are examples of the extensive and varied coverage which this book provides.

In the rapidly changing world of civil aviation, once familiar operators and liveries frequently change or vanish almost overnight. This book is a wonderful wallow in aviation nostalgia which will appeal to all interested in this fascinating international business over recent decades.

It will also provide inspiration for aviation modellers and encourage them to recreate these forgotten liveries on their models.

AIRLINERS WORLDWIDE

Tom Singfield

Interest in the airliners of the world continues to grow and with it demands for better reference material. Now, following on from the highly popular full colour format of *Airlines Worldwide,* comes a companion volume, devoted to the wide variety of types that ply the world's airways.

The author, an air traffic controller, has scoured the world for the illustrations for this book and provided an informative but highly readable reference to each aircraft. From Anglo-French Concorde to DHC Twin Otter, Airbus A340 to Beech 1900D, Douglas Dakota to Boeing 777 – the details of the airliner workhorses of the late 1990s are all there.

Ranging from the humble 15-seat feederliner to the huge Boeing 747-400, the book provides full colour illustrations of the major types, and roams the planet for rare and colourful examples. Detail given includes development, conversions and sub-series, number built and number in service. Also included is a listing of the airlines using each type.

Softback,
240 x 170 mm, 128 pages
135 full colour photographs
1 85780 056 7
Published August 1997
UK £11.95 / US $19.95

Softback
240 x 170 mm, 160 pages
234 colour photographs
1 85780 098 2
Published May 2000
UK £13.95 / US $23.95

CLASSIC AIRLINERS

Tom Singfield

This companion volume to *Airliners Worldwide, Airlines Worldwide* and Airlines Remembered, reviews the specifications, histories and operations of 76 airliner types from the last half century.

The book is illustrated with over 200 outstanding full colour photographs from all around the world, showing the aircraft both in airline service and examples which have been preserved and can still be seen today.

Included are fondly remembered types such as the Lockheed Constellation, Douglas DC-3 and Vickers Viscount, plus some less well-known yet significant types, for instance the Dassault Mercure, Breguet Deux Ponts, Saab Scandia, and VFW-614.

Of course, all the appropriate types from the major manufacturers including Boeing, Douglas, Antonov, Lockheed, Ilyushin, and Tupolev also appear in the book . Classic Airliners offers a wealth of aviation nostalgia for all of those interested in the rapidly changing world of civil aviation.

Softback
240 x 170 mm, c384 pages
c360 full colour photographs
1 85780 103 2
Due to be published Autumn 2000
UK c£18.95 / US c$34.95

AIRLINES WORLDWIDE

B I Hengi

The first edition of this guide was published in 1994 and met a large and appreciative audience. Here could be found details of the major airlines of the world, including base, call-signs and codes, brief history, route structure and types operated or on order.

All essential reading but the major feature of *Airlines Worldwide* was its superb large size full colour photographs providing vibrant detail of the current colour schemes of the world's major airlines.

A second edition followed in 1997 and now three years on this third edition will be eagerly sought by enthusiasts the world over.

The book has once again been completely revised and updated to take into account the fast-changing airline business. As before the book will deal with both the hardware in the shape of the aircraft and the companies which operate them.

In only a short while *Airlines Worldwide* has established itself as a trusted and sought-after reference work.

C000182861

AFFIRMATIONS
FOR
every
day

GILLY PICKUP

summersdale

An Hachette UK Company
www.hachette.co.uk

Summersdale Publishers Ltd
Part of Octopus Publishing Group Limited
Carmelite House
50 Victoria Embankment
LONDON
EC4Y 0DZ
UK

www.summersdale.com

Printed and bound in China

ISBN: 978-1-78685-993-8

Substantial discounts on bulk quantities of Summersdale books are available to corporations, professional associations and other organizations. For details contact general enquiries: telephone: +44 (0) 1243 771107 or email: enquiries@summersdale.com.

To...........................

From......................

Affirmations are short, powerful, positive statements to help you to challenge and overcome negative thoughts. Regularly and sincerely reciting affirmations can bring positive changes into your life.

I CAN DO WHATEVER I PUT MY MIND TO.

Repeat your affirmations out loud. Verbally affirming your hopes and dreams can empower you. When you say "I can," you reassure yourself that your words will become reality.

Every day I develop my constructive habits.

Affirmations are powerful motivators. There is a psychological concept called a "self-fulfilling prophecy". Psychologists have noted that there is a link between belief and actions; if you believe something is likely to come true, you subconsciously change your actions to bring about your prediction. This has been observed in many studies of human behaviour, sometimes yielding a positive effect, sometimes a negative one. Affirmations use the technique of self-fulfilling prophecy in a positive way. Put simply, when you say positive things about yourself, you start to believe them and act accordingly. Say your affirmation two or three times a day whenever it is convenient for you. If you are not in a position to say your affirmation out loud, perhaps because there are other people around, then mentally recite it or write it down.

I AM A POSITIVE
PERSON, AWARE OF
MY POTENTIAL.

Virtually nothing
is impossible in this
world if you just put your
mind to it and maintain
a positive attitude.

Lou Holtz

Everything
I need to
succeed is in
my possession.

It's easy to create your own affirmations. Start by focusing on an area of your life that you would like to improve or change. Perhaps you would like to have more confidence, or would like to be more assertive when you're with people. Write a positive affirmation that will help you improve that area. For example, you might tell yourself – with conviction – that your confidence is soaring.

Make your affirmations short. Four- or five-word statements pack in a lot of power by focusing your desire for improvement on one key area. Plus, they are much easier to remember!

SUCCESS

will come to me.

Always make your affirmations positive. Build your affirmations around what you want to achieve. For instance, instead of saying, "I will not spend my money so quickly," it's much more positive to say, "I make good financial decisions. I save my money." Instead of, "I am not suffering from fear of flying," you could say, "I am completely free from fear of flying." In the second example we replace the negative word "suffering" with the positive, empowering phrase "completely free". Doesn't it feel much better? It's exactly the same message, but reframed in a more positive light.

A POSITIVE ATTITUDE IS
SOMETHING EVERYONE
CAN WORK ON, AND
EVERYONE CAN LEARN
HOW TO EMPLOY IT.

Joan Lunden

Repeat your affirmation. The repetition
will help your subconscious to absorb
your meaning and intent. Regular practice
means you set up a positive daily flow.

Affirmations work because you concentrate on
and repeat whatever it may be that you want to
happen or come into your life. That focus causes
your subconscious to influence your actions,
helping you gravitate toward your goal.

Write or recite your affirmations in the present tense. That way you are telling your mind *this is already happening* and that whatever it is you are saying, thinking or writing is true now.

Begin your affirmations with "I" or "My". When you recite an affirmation, you are making a statement about yourself. This is because it is only through changing your own mindset and actions that you can change your situation.

Set attainable goals, especially if you are just starting to practise affirmations. Small steps are sustainable steps. There is nothing wrong with aiming high, but it is important to grow your practice in a natural way.

I appreciate my body and I have a brilliant mind.

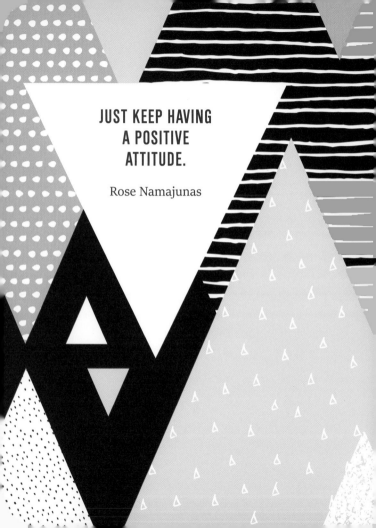

JUST KEEP HAVING
A POSITIVE
ATTITUDE.

Rose Namajunas

Use your own voice and phrasing when writing or reciting affirmations. Don't feel you have to write them in a stylized manner for them to work! You are writing/speaking them for yourself and for your own benefit. Be comfortable with the words and phrases you use. Your affirmations can be silly or colourful; they can even be thoughts that no one else understands but you. When you write your affirmations in your own words, you connect with them more deeply.

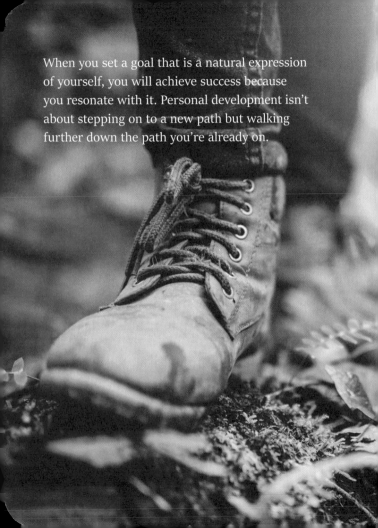

When you set a goal that is a natural expression
of yourself, you will achieve success because
you resonate with it. Personal development isn't
about stepping on to a new path but walking
further down the path you're already on.

I ALWAYS
KNOW WHAT
I SHOULD
DO IN ANY
SITUATION.

I APPROVE OF MYSELF
AND EVERYTHING
THAT I DO.

Avoid using the word "try". Its meaning is very different from "do". For example, the affirmation "I study for one hour every day" is more effective than "I try to study for one hour every day."

Affirmations can build on elements of your life that are going well. They do not have to solely focus on inviting new situations into your world. Think about your positive attributes and things that already work well for you. What do you like about yourself and what are you grateful for? Include these in your affirmations too. We often forget to give ourselves credit for things that we like about ourselves, so when writing affirmations, remember to describe some things that you already appreciate about yourself. This will reinforce your positive feelings about who you are and you will be more open to accepting affirmations that describe who you would like to become.

I am the sum
of my thoughts.
That is why
my thoughts
are positive.

When you recite or write
your affirmations, do it
wholeheartedly. Be 100 per
cent positive that what you are
asking for is what you want.
When you believe something,
you will receive it.

Create the highest,
grandest vision possible
for your life, because you
become what you believe.

Oprah Winfrey

I BELIEVE IN MY

abilities

AND I FIND IT EASY TO

express

MYSELF.

Remember that your thoughts are always
under your control. When you think
in a positive way, your thoughts create
your reality. If you dwell on a negative
thought, you will still be using the power
of affirmations and self-fulfilling prophecy.
Recognize the thought and reject it,
consciously switching to a positive thought.

I AM GRATEFUL
FOR ALL THE

GOOD
THINGS

I HAVE IN MY LIFE.

When you experience negative thoughts, your body reacts too. If you are struggling to move on mentally from your negative thinking then try this mindfulness exercise. Take a moment to relax your body. Through mindful breathing, use the out-breath to release tension in your body, as well as any negative thinking. If it makes it easier, you could imagine negative thoughts leaving your body with the out-breath.

CONSTANT REPETITION CARRIES CONVICTION.

Robert Collier

The most effective way to reinforce positive affirmations is to recite them aloud. If you find that niggling negative thoughts creep into your mind, or realize you are using any negative words, say a positive affirmation out loud to counteract the negativity. If it's easier, then record the affirmation on your phone using the voice memo feature. Set a notification to sound every hour and repeat your affirmation when you hear the ring.

Use your affirmations
to overcome self-sabotaging
behaviour. Sometimes, when we do
not truly believe that we can achieve a
goal, our negative mindset starts to affect
our actions. We might procrastinate, put off
even starting a new goal or start to express
frustration and negative self-worth. Use
affirmations to break through this
mental block and change your
behaviour to positive,
effective actions.

Positive thinking makes you feel happier. Happier people experience reduced stress levels which is linked to better cardiovascular health.

Start today! Your subconscious mind translates your thoughts and ideas into real life, so keep those feelings upbeat and know that good things are on their way. It will happen if you let it happen. Start to welcome positivity into your life now!

DON'T FORGET TO TELL YOURSELF POSITIVE THINGS DAILY. YOU MUST LOVE YOURSELF INTERNALLY TO GLOW EXTERNALLY.

Hannah Bronfman

I AM ABOVE NEGATIVE THOUGHTS AND ACTIONS.

You can use the positive phrasing from your affirmations to improve even your everyday and commonplace thoughts. Always phrase your thoughts in the affirmative. Instead of saying "I do not want to miss that train" turn it round and say "I will catch that train." Avoid saying, "I am worried that I will not do well in my exam." Say instead, "I know that I will do well in my exam." This positive outlook will improve your mood and reduce your daily worries.

Our thoughts are the most powerful things we have, so choose to make them constructive. It is sometimes too easy to think the worst about ourselves, to imagine perhaps that others think badly of us or say less than flattering things about us. We cannot change what others feel or say, but we can change what we feel and think. Think positively.

HE WHO SAYS
HE CAN AND
HE WHO SAYS HE
CAN'T ARE BOTH
USUALLY RIGHT.

Confucius

Pervasive and consistent negative thoughts are a form of self-sabotage. If your thoughts run along the lines of, "I'll never find myself a job that I'm happy in. I'm going to be stuck in this dead-end job forever," that is probably exactly what will happen. Instead recite the affirmation, "A job with my name on it is very close." Be excited as you wait for your new job to come along. Visualize what you will feel like when you are told that this new job is yours. You will then feel less defeated and more motivated to search for new opportunities.

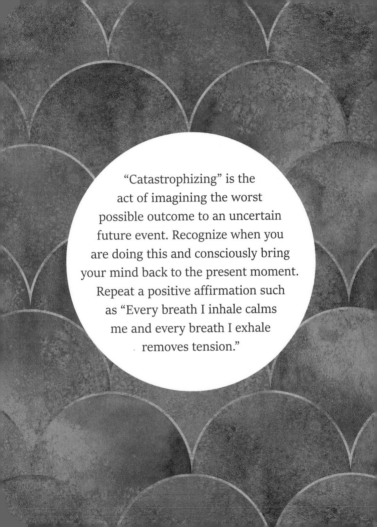

"Catastrophizing" is the act of imagining the worst possible outcome to an uncertain future event. Recognize when you are doing this and consciously bring your mind back to the present moment. Repeat a positive affirmation such as "Every breath I inhale calms me and every breath I exhale removes tension."

A POSITIVE ATTITUDE CAN REALLY MAKE DREAMS COME TRUE - IT DID FOR ME.

David Bailey

When you find yourself catastrophizing, say "stop" to cease those thoughts. Consciously think about a positive outcome to the situation, or even a less-negative option. Believe in yourself and know that you can overcome your tendency to fear the worst.

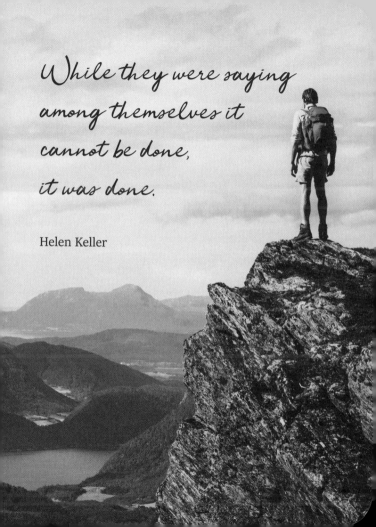

While they were saying among themselves it cannot be done, it was done.

Helen Keller

I focus on what I **can do,** not on what I can't.

Accompany your positive affirmations with strong, positive feelings and actions. Be mindful of the actions you take to achieve your goals and acknowledge them to yourself. When you have worked hard or taken a step toward achieving your goals, say to yourself, "I always take positive actions to achieve my aims." It feels good to have our hard work recognized – even by ourselves! When you feel that your work is productive you are more likely to stay energized and motivated and continue that good work.

Learning to think positively is like exercising a muscle: the more you use it, the stronger it will become. Some days may feel easier than others to keep on the side of positivity, but persevere and you'll get there!

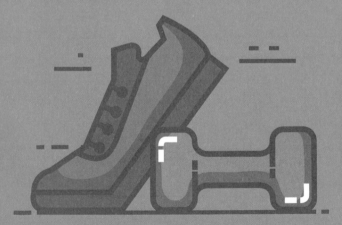

Affirmations can help improve your self-esteem.
Tell yourself, "I am fabulous just the way I am."
With time and repetition, you will believe it and
feel more fabulous with every passing day.

Energize your life from the inside out.
On a practical level that means being aware
of what you eat, enjoying balanced meals
and getting enough sleep. On a mental and
spiritual level, it means energizing yourself
with affirmations and positive thinking.
Think positive thoughts as often as you can.
Visualize yourself brimming with energy, leaping
out of bed in the mornings and embracing the
day. Know without a doubt that if you really
believe your goal is achievable and you are
determined to make it happen, you will shape
your life to make your dreams a reality.

I have
unlimited
energy
for life.

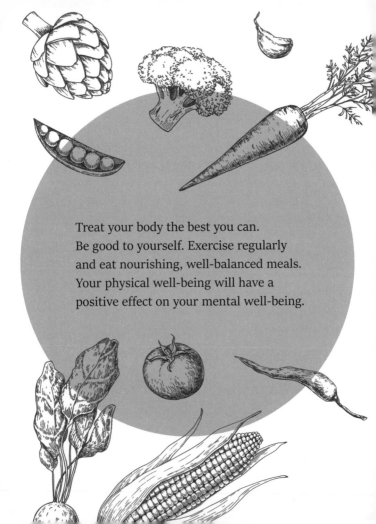

Treat your body the best you can.
Be good to yourself. Exercise regularly
and eat nourishing, well-balanced meals.
Your physical well-being will have a
positive effect on your mental well-being.

I LOOK AFTER MYSELF
AND MY BODY IS
STRONG AND HEALTHY.

Say "good morning" to every part of your body. Breathe deeply and, starting with your toes, move your attention up through your body, blessing every section as you go. Really feel that strong life force moving all the way up through every part of your being. You will feel so much more alive after you have done this. You will be energized and raring to make the day as good as you possibly can.

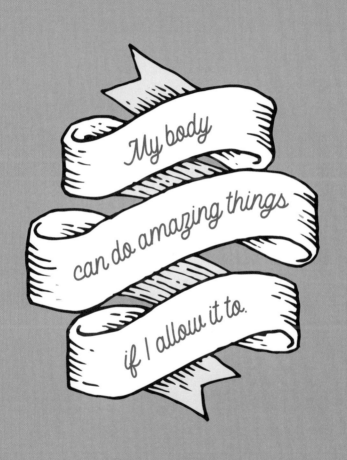

I become more
knowledgeable

EVERY
DAY.

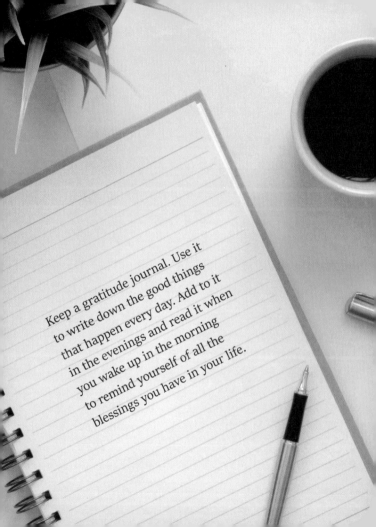

Keep a gratitude journal. Use it to write down the good things that happen every day. Add to it in the evenings and read it when you wake up in the morning to remind yourself of all the blessings you have in your life.

I AM BRIMMING WITH

energy

AND OVERFLOWING WITH

joy.

ADOPTING A POSITIVE
ATTITUDE CAN WORK
WONDERS TO ADDING
YEARS TO YOUR LIFE,
A SPRING TO YOUR
STEP, A SPARKLE
TO YOUR EYE.

Christie Brinkley

When you hold on to thoughts and
possessions that you do not use any
more they can create blocks in your
life. Clutter, whether in your mind or
your home, is stagnant energy. Less
clutter makes you feel more organized.
You will feel freer and more focused.
Get rid of possessions that you do
not love, or do not need any more.
If they are still in good condition
or working order, give them to a
charity, because there is undoubtedly
someone out there who *will* love them.
Develop a healthy attitude toward
your possessions and appreciate
that when you are freed from your
clutter, you have the physical and
mental capacity to embrace new
items and experiences in life.

IN THE RIGHT LIGHT, AT THE RIGHT TIME, EVERYTHING IS EXTRAORDINARY.

Aaron Rose

If ever you don't feel like you're in the right headspace to read or write your affirmation, try deep breathing for a few minutes. It has a restful, calming effect on your mind and body. Inhale by expanding your abdominal muscles and draw the air into your diaphragm. Hold for a couple of seconds, then exhale as slowly as you feel comfortable with. Repeat three times. This exercise, when practised regularly, is relaxing and calming. A relaxed mind accepts suggestions much more easily than a mind which flutters from one thought to the next.

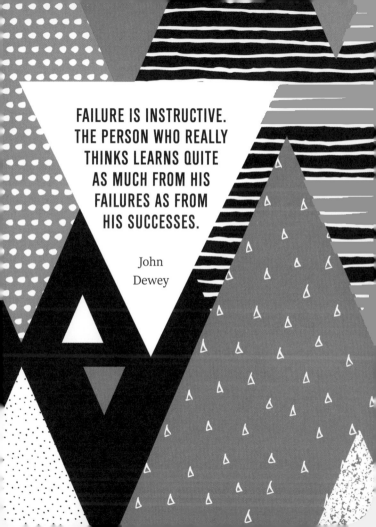

FAILURE IS INSTRUCTIVE.
THE PERSON WHO REALLY
THINKS LEARNS QUITE
AS MUCH FROM HIS
FAILURES AS FROM
HIS SUCCESSES.

John
Dewey

EVERY DAY I FEEL
MORE AND MORE
CONFIDENT
AND READY TO
FACE THE WORLD.

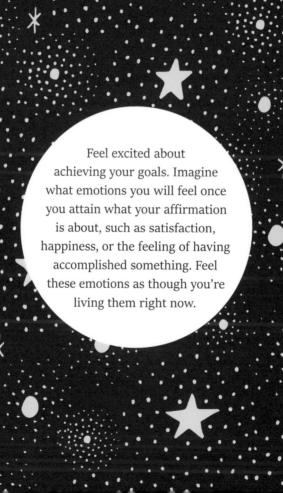

Feel excited about achieving your goals. Imagine what emotions you will feel once you attain what your affirmation is about, such as satisfaction, happiness, or the feeling of having accomplished something. Feel these emotions as though you're living them right now.

I am
PATIENT,
TOLERANT
and
DIPLOMATIC.

Louise Hay

Affirmations work best when you are working toward specific goals, so write your statements down and reread them regularly; use your affirmations to reinforce and work toward them. Reciting or reading your daily affirmations will help to manifest your goals. Check in with yourself after a year, removing any goals you have achieved and setting new ones. New year is the perfect time to do this as we are accustomed to setting our New Year's resolutions.

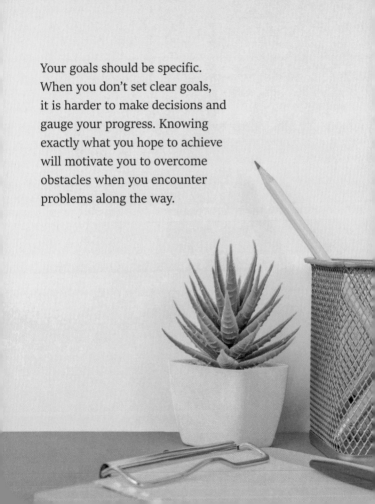

Your goals should be specific.
When you don't set clear goals,
it is harder to make decisions and
gauge your progress. Knowing
exactly what you hope to achieve
will motivate you to overcome
obstacles when you encounter
problems along the way.

I WAKE UP IN THE
MORNING FEELING
HAPPY AND ENTHUSIASTIC
ABOUT THE DAY AHEAD.

Recite or read your affirmations after you wake up and before you go to bed. That way you start and end your day with a clear vision of your goals.

Keep your affirmations close at hand. Pin them to the wall, write them on post it notes and stick them on your bathroom mirror, or get a magnet and put them on your fridge door. The more you say and think them, the more readily your mind will accept them.

If you want abundance and affluence to enter your life, you have to think in terms of abundance and affluence. Focus on what you want; make plans, set goals and reaffirm to yourself that you deserve prosperity. Don't rely on the first words that come into your mind; use language that fires you up, words that mean a lot to you. Use exciting words, words that encourage you and spur you on. Bring passion into your vocabulary. From today, open yourself up to ever-increasing prosperity.

Confidence
comes
naturally
to me.

Always go with your passions. Never ask yourself if it's realistic or not.

Deepak Chopra

If you think of your mind as a garden, you know that there is only so much space for things to grow. Plant lots of positive "seeds" and then you can see that there is no room left for negative weeds to flourish. The more positive seeds you plant, the more positive flowers there will be. So, the next time a negative thought dares to enter your lovely mind-garden, cut it out. It's easiest to do this when it is still a seedling; a niggling worry or concern. As soon as you dig that negative thought out, plant a new positive thought.

I HAVE BEEN GIVEN ENDLESS

talents

WHICH I WILL UTILIZE

today.

Don't use excuses as reasons for not doing or attempting something. For example, it is simply an excuse to say, "If I had more time then I would write a novel." Or, "I won't progress in work, because I'm not smart enough." Excuses are mental obstacles. Focus on finding the solution to your current issue. For example, you could say, "I will find 30 minutes a day to write my novel." Believe in yourself and the power of your mindset. Stay positive!

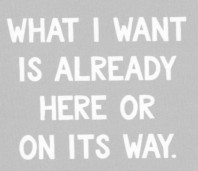

WHAT I WANT
IS ALREADY
HERE OR
ON ITS WAY.

What you create is what you get.
Life reflects back to you what you think
and how you act. If you are not happy with
your current circumstances, use your daily
affirmation practice to help you change.

It is easy to blame others – your parents, work colleagues, perhaps even the whole world – for any difficult situation you may find yourself in. Blaming others can feel "safer" than taking responsibility for a bad result or situation. Remember that you can only learn and improve from failure if you acknowledge the mistakes you might have made. Though a situation may not always be in your control and you might feel inclined to fault others for it, blame is destructive and toxic to our peace of mind and health. Consciously acknowledging and releasing your feelings of blame allows the energy to flow though and out of your energy field, clearing toxicity, leaving you feeling more peaceful and allowing your body to release, relax and heal. If you are a "blamer", make a decision to stop right now and repeat the following affirmation over and over until you firmly believe it. Vibrate it. Feel the words resonate through your entire body.

I forgive
those who have
troubled me in
the past and
peacefully detach
from them.

I am
ready
to face the
day with
confidence.

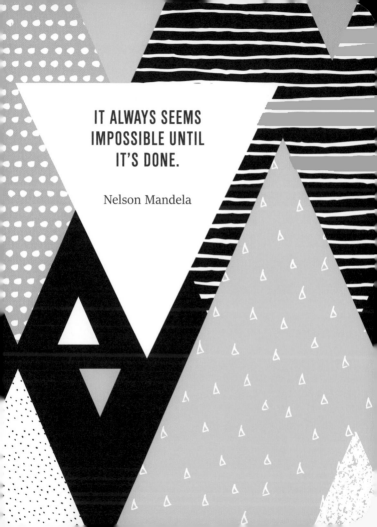

IT ALWAYS SEEMS
IMPOSSIBLE UNTIL
IT'S DONE.

Nelson Mandela

Focus on the potential benefits of the situation when you are faced with an obstacle. For instance, if the train you were scheduled to take is delayed, use the extra time you have for yourself by listening to music or a podcast, reading a book or phoning a friend.

Challenges are opportunities to

IMPROVE

or change.

When life seems to consist of one challenge after another and you journey through times that are less than easy, keep in mind that this will only amount to a short section of your life. Everyone faces their own ups and downs; everyone has hurdles to jump every now and then. Know that difficulties are moving out of your way and keep faith that better times will soon be with you. When you focus on the outcome instead of the problem you will find a solution. Regard any problems as springboards to new ideas, and remember that the last time you encountered difficulties, a solution appeared. This too shall pass. Include an affirmation in your practice to give you strength in challenging times, perhaps telling yourself, "I can get through anything."

I AM CHANGING
MYSELF, MY THINKING
AND MY LIFE

FOR THE
BETTER.

LEAP AND THE NET WILL APPEAR.

Zen proverb

Decide that from now on you will deal calmly with any problems that crop up. You will not waste time on negative emotions such as anger but instead focus on positively and confidently finding a solution. Know within yourself that you always solve any trials and tribulations ably and with ease. Affirm that you will solve your problems without difficulty as long as you stay calm and relaxed and know that a solution will present itself to you.

PEARLS
don't lie on the
SEASHORE.
If you want one,
you must
DIVE
for it.

Chinese proverb

Never give up on whatever it is you wish to achieve. Know that you have not yet explored every option and keep telling yourself that you will overcome any problem.

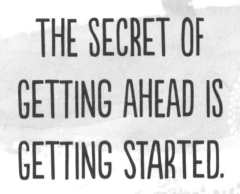

THE SECRET OF GETTING AHEAD IS GETTING STARTED.

Mark Twain

You embody your thoughts. Repeating positive affirmations about yourself will help self-confidence fill your mind and then your actions. You are always in control of your actions.

Share your positivity with those around you.
Be nice to those you meet. Give them a smile or
a compliment. Know that you attract positive
people and events into your life and choose
to see beauty and joy wherever you look.

SUCCESS IS MY DRIVING FORCE.

EVERY DAY IN EVERY
WAY I AM BECOMING MORE
PROSPEROUS. I ALWAYS
HAVE WHATEVER
I NEED.

Take a moment to consider: what is actually good right now? What is good in your life? It could be that you are safe, healthy, and have a job you like. Whatever it might be, name a few things, recognize them and keep those thoughts close for a short time. Every time you see something positive, take a moment to be grateful and to appreciate your blessings.

It can feel like an effort to keep thinking positively, especially in the face of challenging situations. Like any goal, the key is to stick with it. Don't give up. Repeat your affirmations daily. Even if you find yourself dwelling on negative thoughts, you can look for ways to minimize negative self-talk and encourage a more optimistic outlook. One way to help positivity flow in your life is to take time to do things you enjoy. Another way to encourage the continual flow of positive thoughts is to take the focus away from yourself and do something nice for another person.

I can
handle all
problems
with ease.

Multiple
opportunities
are always there
for me and I
take advantage
of them.

For every achievement that is outstanding, the common ingredient is determination. Do not quit, be persistent. Sometimes determination is trying again, sometimes it means finding a different path. Create an affirmation to reinforce your determination.

I AM
GRATEFUL FOR
EXPERIENCES
THAT HELP
ME LEARN.

Meditate on your affirmations. Close your eyes, breathe deeply, try to shut out the rest of the world and think about your affirmations. Slowly and calmly repeat the words, thinking about what each one means to you. Visualize the positive feelings you want to create or the goals you want to achieve each time you say your affirmation. If you are new to meditation, start by taking a few slow, deep breaths and trying to clear your mind. You probably won't get all the noise out the first few times and that's alright. The simple act of trying can still have positive effects.

When you stand around on the edge of life, being indecisive and unsure of what to do next, things will probably rumble on as they are without a lot of change coming your way. You have to make the first move. Say with gusto, "I will do it" – whatever your aim is – and you will be so much more successful than if you had said, "Well, I'd like to do it, but I'm not sure that I will manage." You will get results.

Love yourself. It is
important to stay positive
because beauty comes
from the inside out.

Jenn Proske

De-stress on a regular basis. Affirmations go a long way to helping you bear a bad situation, but sometimes your body and mind need you to simply release the tension. This could take the form of a short walk, getting a massage, meditating or even singing aloud when you are in the bath or shower.

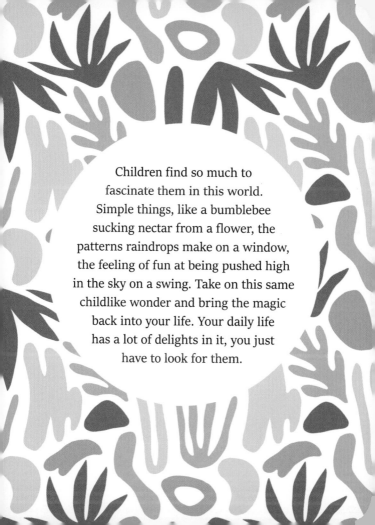

Children find so much to fascinate them in this world. Simple things, like a bumblebee sucking nectar from a flower, the patterns raindrops make on a window, the feeling of fun at being pushed high in the sky on a swing. Take on this same childlike wonder and bring the magic back into your life. Your daily life has a lot of delights in it, you just have to look for them.

Only I can
change my life.
No one can
do it for me.

Carol Burnett

My whole being
overflows with

JOY.

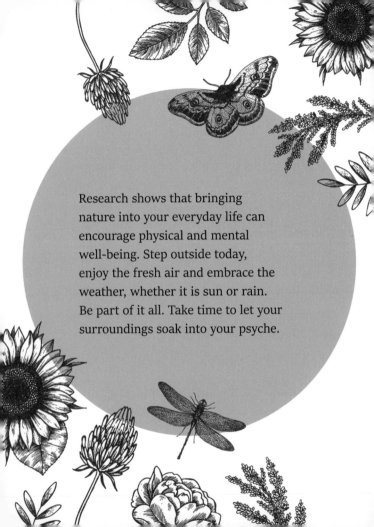

Research shows that bringing nature into your everyday life can encourage physical and mental well-being. Step outside today, enjoy the fresh air and embrace the weather, whether it is sun or rain. Be part of it all. Take time to let your surroundings soak into your psyche.

THERE IS ONLY ONE WAY TO AVOID CRITICISM:

DO NOTHING, SAY NOTHING AND BE NOTHING.

Aristotle

Remember that repetition is the key when it comes to affirmations. If you are trying to change a belief that you have held firm for the last ten or fifteen years, then it will likely require persistence to change.

I RELEASE NEGATIVE
THOUGHTS AND
EMBRACE OPTIMISM.

Just as you exercise your body to keep it supple, flexible and healthy, you should do the same with your mind. Imagination is the key to problem-solving, and when you imagine your life as you want it to be, you are creating mental pictures. The more vivid you can make these pictures the more powerful the results of your affirmations will be. Giving your imagination a positive-thinking workout will make you feel good.

My work
is
enjoyable
and
satisfies me
completely.

We all experience mood dips, sometimes even when it seems everything is going well. Remind yourself that you are not just enough, you are amazing. You are a light that shines.

I TAP INTO A
WELLSPRING OF
INNER HAPPINESS
ANY TIME I
WANT TO.

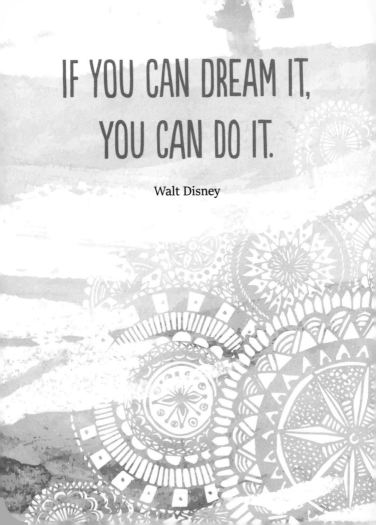

Being kind makes you more inclined to
be grateful for things in your life. If you
sometimes find it difficult to think positive
thoughts and find something to be thankful for,
then do a good deed for someone else. It could
be something small and simple like buying
someone a cup of coffee or listening if they need
someone to talk to. You will help your friend or
loved one and you will also feel good yourself.

TODAY IS A NEW DAY.
YOU WILL GET OUT
OF IT JUST WHAT
YOU PUT INTO IT.

Mary Pickford

Be as kind to yourself as you would be to others. You are a great person and you deserve your respect. If you are someone who often compares yourself negatively to others, add an affirmation to your daily practice. Tell yourself that you are unique and wonderful.

I deserve self-praise and I am open to receiving it.

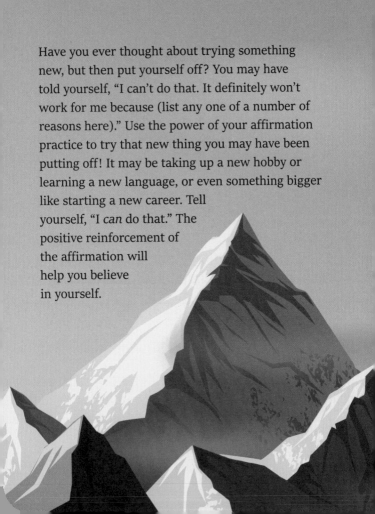

Have you ever thought about trying something new, but then put yourself off? You may have told yourself, "I can't do that. It definitely won't work for me because (list any one of a number of reasons here)." Use the power of your affirmation practice to try that new thing you may have been putting off! It may be taking up a new hobby or learning a new language, or even something bigger like starting a new career. Tell yourself, "I *can* do that." The positive reinforcement of the affirmation will help you believe in yourself.

We always may be what
we might have been.

Adelaide Anne Procter

Creative
energy

FLOWS

through me.

WHEN YOU ARE
ENTHUSIASTIC ABOUT
WHAT YOU DO, YOU FEEL
THIS POSITIVE ENERGY.
IT'S VERY SIMPLE.

Paulo Coelho

Affirmations work wonders, but that doesn't mean you should hang around waiting for things to happen. Live for the now and be mindful of the rich present moment that is open to you.

Small actions, like smiling, laughing or singing – even when you don't feel like it – can trick your brain into feeling happy and relieve feelings of stress. Another plus point about smiling in particular is that it takes fewer muscles to do so than it does to frown! If you want to sing aloud, it doesn't matter one bit whether you have a good singing voice or are totally tone deaf, or if you can't remember the words of the song you're singing. If something is enjoyable to you and it makes you feel better, then embrace it.

WHEN YOU THINK
POSITIVE, GOOD
THINGS HAPPEN.

Matt Kemp

I FEEL JOY
AND PEACE IN
THIS MOMENT.

Having a positive
relationship with your body
is effective in improving the
quality of your daily life.
Invest in yourself by getting
enough exercise and sleep.

Affirmations can even help you with your love life! It can be hard to take the first step when looking for love, especially if you are shy or dogged with low self-esteem. Use affirmations to reassure yourself that you are deserving of love.

I have a
lot to offer.
I deserve
love &
respect.

WITH THE NEW DAY
COMES NEW STRENGTH
AND NEW THOUGHTS.

Eleanor Roosevelt

When you lack motivation and feel that you want to do more with your life but feel stuck in a rut, keep believing in yourself. Know that the answer is right in front of you even if you can't see what it is at this moment.

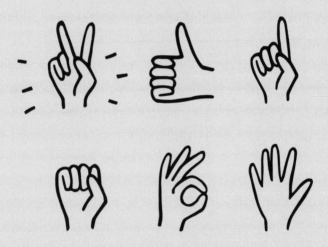

I AM
ENERGETIC,
MOTIVATED
AND
READY
TO GO!

LIFE TAKES CARE
OF ALL MY NEEDS.

You may have set clear goals and chosen specific and focused affirmations but haven't seen results yet. Sometimes, life gets in the way of itself! You may not currently understand how you will achieve your aims, but it doesn't mean that it won't happen. Believe in yourself and remember that there is always a way. Trust in the process of life and be aware that nothing in the past or present interferes with the divine flow. Life is happening to you now.

There are lots of resources to help you
develop your affirmations. Besides those
in this book, you could go to classes,
watch videos or look at affirmative
imagery. Try several options and you
will find what particularly inspires you.

I am always
inspired and
productive and
continue to
develop in my
chosen path.

I AM
STRONGER
THAN I
THINK.

Recognize that you matter and constantly remind yourself that you deserve all that is good in life. This is not an act of selfishness but an act of self-love. When you appreciate yourself people you meet will recognize your core of self-respect. If you assume that people won't treat you with respect, then you might end up in a situation where this is the case. However, if you radiate your own self-respect when you are around other people, they are far more likely to match the positivity you show to them. You deserve to be treated well, by yourself and by others.

If you find yourself thinking something like, "I can't do anything properly," replace it with a phrase that is much more realistic, such as, "Sometimes I make mistakes, but I learn from them."

I AM

bursting

WITH GREAT IDEAS
AND I OFFER A

unique

PERSPECTIVE.

YOU CAN'T JUST SIT
THERE AND WAIT FOR
PEOPLE TO GIVE YOU
THAT GOLDEN DREAM.
YOU'VE GOT TO GET
OUT THERE AND
MAKE IT HAPPEN
FOR YOURSELF.

Diana Ross

Find out who you are and
be that person... find that
truth, live that truth and
everything else will come.

Ellen DeGeneres

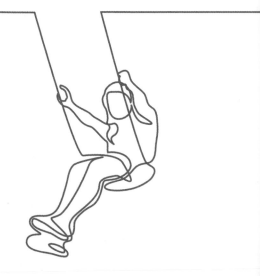

I radiate love and respect and in return I get love and respect.

If you're interested in finding out more about our books, find us on Facebook at **Summersdale Publishers** and follow us on Twitter at **@Summersdale**.

www.summersdale.com